TURNING ...POINTS
BY JOB ELIZES

(Empty Dreams)
First Published, 1968
Reissue, 2012

Job Elizes, Sr.
1910-1992

"A people who, two thousand years ago when they were primitive, with their bare hands and creative minds --without foreign aid --built the famous Banawe rice terraces, considered one of the engineering wonders of the world, have no reason in this twentieth century, to beg from other nations." -CELSO A. CARUNUNGAN (Well-known Filipino author.)

Self-Publisher

Tatay Jobo Elizes, son of late Job Elizes Sr., was born in Manila, Philippines, in 1934, now retiree, based in NY, busy writing and self-publishing as a hobby and involved in piglets dispersal programs for livelihood projects in the Philippines via the internet.

ISBN-13-978: 1481188883   ISBN-10: 1481188887

Front cover picture: Teacher's Camp, Baguio City, Philippines

Notes:

Turning Points is a short story by my late father, Job Elizes Sr (1910-1991), published in the Phi8lippines in 1968. As there are no more copies available, I am publishing this new reissues, circa 2009 and 2012. The 2009 re-issue is size 6x9 inches while this one is size 5x8 inches. This is after almost 40 years.

The main character in the story is **Juanito** who is witnessing reforms and changes that are occurring in the Philippines based on his fantasy, as some sorts of turning points in history. The social ills facing the country in 1960s are still the same and have never really changed. I just thought it only appropriate to re-issue this book today. The original book is retained in its entirety, except that I added subtitle, **Empty Dreams**.

My father said this book is suggested long-range solution to the problem of peace and order. If elementary education is compulsory, and all the school children starting at 4th Grade are required to memorize, ingest, learn by heart (with the aid of spaced repetition, mental osmosis, and sleep-learning if feasible) the following gems of thought by aristocrats of the mind, the full impact of their meaning and message can become permanent part and parcel of the child's thinking and philosophy of life (see Selected Quotations).

Dedication

My father was not able to dedicate this book to anybody. On his behalf and in his memory, I dedicate this book to all my brothers and sisters and their individual families and my own family, consisting of my wife, **Cora, my children, Tetchie, Chevy & Abeth, Marie & Bimbo, and my grandchildren, Karin & Aung, Noelle, Chad, Marjo, Jeb, Marvin & Marty, and great-grandchild Jason Win Aung.**

Acknowledgment:

My brother, Bobby Elizes drew the pictures. circa 1968.

Selected Quotations:

1. "The child is the father of the man." -Wordsworth

2. "In the sweat of thy face shall thou eat bread." - The Bible

3. "Reverence for life is the basic element of human behavior." -Schweitzer

4. "A man's home however humble is his castle: The winds may enter, the rains may enter, but the King shall not enter." - Lord Chatham

5. "I disagree in what you say but I shall defend to the death your right to say it." - Voltaire

6. "The right to be heard does not carry with it the right to be taken seriously." - Humphrey

7. "No man is good enough to govern another without the latter's consent." - Lincoln

8. "Ignorance of the law excuses no one." -Selden

9. "I campaign for election in my district from county to county alone in a car driven by my wife." - PM Atlee

10. "I sought my soul, my soul I did not see; I sought my God, my God eluded me; I sought my brother, I found all three." - Anonymous

Content in Chapters

Preface

Whether the Philippine nation can be great again, on the assumption that it had been great before and is now no longer great; or whether this nation can be great, assuming it has never been great, have one thing in common: this nation is not great. It is far from being great. In fact, it is facing a crisis.

No one seems to deny that this nation can be great. It has the potentials galore for greatness. It has vast natural resources, fertile arable oil, rich forests, rich mines, pleasant climate almost the whole year round, more than 30 million people, hundreds of thousands of college graduates, with a college population studying in the many colleges and universities of the land greater than that of some of the more advanced countries of even greater size and population, with a democratic form of government whose foundations were firmly laid out by her former occupying country, the USA, the greatest country in the world.

The Filipinos are inherently creative as those of other countries. According to noted writer **Celso Carunungan,** "More than 2000 years ago a primitive people, without any foreign aid but with their bare hands and creative minds, constructed the awe-inspiring rice terraces of Bontoc, one of the many everlasting wonders of the world." In spite of these great potentials, natural as well as human, why is it then that this nation is facing a great crisis?

"INDIFERENCE AT ALL LEVELS LED TO THIS CRISIS," said Manila's leading newspaper front page editorial. What are the symptoms of this crisis? To name a few, according to the editorial:

(a) Respect for the law, for civic order and for decency has broken down. Violence already at a high rate is rising. Faith in the authorities no longer exists. For many, high and low, the law exists only to be broken or circumvented.

(b) Success of smuggling.

(c)Perennial rice shortage; the deteriorating service of the water supply; the deteriorating service of our national railroad, the mail service, garbage collection and other essential public services.

May I add,

(d) Cynicism, or the attitude and thinking of the majority of the people, in all levels of society: government employees and private citizens, mostly all embracing the philosophy of "unahan" (cutting in line), "lamangan" (cheating), and "gulangan" (bullying and brute force). These three usual tenets in the pursuit of livelihood are being followed by the people, as pointed out vividly by a great magazine editorial. Is there a solution to these problems somewhere, sometime, somehow? Nobody seems to deny that there is a solution. Every problem has a solution; perhaps the only thing that has no solution is death and this nation, thanks to Almighty God, is still young and far from dying. In one university in Manila, the enrolment is staggering 62,000! As Mr. William Greaves, noted psychologist pointed out and proved: "The wealth of a nation consists of the creative words and ideas freely expressed by its people," this country with its vast natural and human resources have no reason to be threatened by a crisis.

There must be turning points.

When one is sick in bed for a number of days under treatment by a physician, there is a time during this sickness when the doctor could say that the crisis is over and there has been a turning point for the better. And the sick man would be on the way to recovery provided no complications will set in and the instructions of the doctor will be followed religiously. Similarly, when a man sets up a business and works hard to make his business successful, there is a time after a few years of hard work when the businessman will have determined that the turning point for the better has been reached. When the business has already come out of the red and the ledger shows a little bit of comfortable profit, then the businessman can safely say that his business can be carried out profitably provided the members of the organization follow the regimen or set of rules in running the business, formed at great pains, many of them through trial and error and therefore "forged like steel on the anvil of experience." Again, to cite another example, when a man is trying to creatively solve a knotty problem and he has been trying to find the solution for quite a long time, trying this and that solution, or a part of this or a part of that solution, seeking the advice and help of relatives and friends, there is a time when he discovers that the problem is on the way to a solution, or in other words the turning point for the better has been reached.

The purpose of this novelette is to try to point out how the turning points for the better of some of the pressing problems plaguing our Philippine nation today can be reached. It must be pointed out at the outset that the turning point in a crisis is reached only after sometime, perhaps a long time of constant, continuous and relentless creative efforts towards the solution of the problem. Perhaps we are naïve in saying so, but we have to say it nonetheless. No successful business was built overnight or as they say, "Rome was not built in a day." Aside from realizing that to reach the turning point requires constant effort and patience, one must be prepared for complications and relapses that will set back the timetable to reach the turning point. The saying that, "if the principle is right the rest will be a matter of details" does not hold water when trying to solve the problems facing the Philippines. In fact, in the solution of our problems, it is better for one to desist from mere principles and shallow generalizations, but instead stick to specific techniques and methodology as developed by recognized creative thinkers. Again, in trying to reach the turning point one should tell himself that, "there is not a job in the world that cannot be done better than it is being done. A man is not doing the best he can for the company that employs him, the people he serves, or for the world, if he goes through life without looking for that better way."

Moreover in trying to solve the problem, if the solution does not appear when one pursues the usual methods of solution, one should try the unusual methods. And lastly, in trying to reach the turning point, the energies and talents of the good people of this country must be solicited. We must impress upon our citizenry the meaning of the great words of **Edmund Burke:** "the only thing necessary for the triumph of evil is for good men to do nothing." Let us try to arouse the so called "constructive discontent" in our people and make them to cry out the so called "small voice in the wilderness," and perhaps if more people will each have a feeble voice but if all the feeble voices will cry out in unison, the resulting voice will be a ROAR, loud and clear, strong and demanding, whose command will not only be heard but will have to be obeyed.

To solve the grave and pressing problems of our country we must accept and rely upon the fact that "we have creative individuals with the passionate desire to serve," in the words of Rolando Carbonell, a noted poet and thinker of the younger generation. He states further "when President Marcos, in an extemporaneous speech before the Rotarians recently, called upon the creative minority to lead in the solution of the problems facing the country today, he was in effect providing a clue to the strategy of our national development. As a matter of fact, the same sentiment has been expressed in his inaugural address: **(quote) The attainment of national greatness means releasing to the fullest extent the creative energies and raising the level of competence to solve the great problems confronting us today through our OWN efforts. Let us remember that a nation can only be as great as the creative leaders and people that comprise it (quote)."**

"The first law of creative success is to quit looking outside ourselves for solutions to our problems," said Elmer G. Letterman, famous inspirational writer.

Educate the heart - curriculum subject

First and foremost of these solutions, perhaps because it will take the greatest length of time -probably a generation or two -is the inclusion of a subject in the curriculum of our schools which may be called **Education For Harmonious Human Relations or Education For Community Living. Or, call it Character Education.** The great defect in our educational system is that while the mind is trained in the **three R's** there is not a single subject to **educate the heart.** True enough there are certain flimsy, superficial attempts to educate the heart of the school child through good manners and right conduct (so called) but not effectively, merely taught optionally in very short time periods, in generalities and principles but hardly by specifics. If we invest now in the education of the heart, we cannot fail to gather the fruits of our labor in about 10, 15 or even 20 years to change the cynicism of our people today. This is very important according to Fr. Jaime Bulatao, well-known psycho-therapist, "one of the main stumbling blocks to a nation's socio-economic progress is the attitude of the citizen itself. ---The real crisis is within man himself."

Someone said people are like rough pebbles thrown into the revolving drum of life. Their rough edges will be eventually smoothened. The is the negative approach or laissez faire philosophy which resignedly accepts our present chaos. This process of "natural" smoothening of the rough pebbles takes a long time, and in many cases, the friction caused by the contact between the mutually rough pebbles or between rough and smooth pebbles, had resulted in conflict, tragedy, and misery. Let us remember to pre-polish the rough edges of man's character by teaching him the art of harmonious human relations, before throwing him into the revolving drum of life. If we can systematically "heart-wash" every child there will no necessity of finding for our youth the so-called substitutes for violence. Wordsworth said, "The child is the father of the man." Invest in the child's up-bringing and surely reap the rewards in ten to fifteen years time. No less than a former Secretary of Education stated that, "not only is the development of the character he most important aim of education; character education is more important than all other subjects combined."

Revamp Government Procedures -Assembly Line Method.

My next suggestion is the revamping of the government procedures in favor of assembly line method. In other words, let war be declared against red tape! If the public is contemptuous of the service rendered by government employees, it is because of the red tape being practiced by the government bureaus and offices. In fact, many bureaucrats have become geniuses in the art of red tape. To cite an example: A private car parked in accordance with law was bumped by a taxi through the carelessness of the taxi driver, admittedly, under oath, and corroborated by a policeman, who happened to be on duty nearby. The complaint was filed before the authorities. But because of red tape, the just compensation to pay only for the actual damage to the car has not been paid after 8 months of postponement and re-postponement of the hearings due to the alibis of the taxi drivers attorney, and sanctioned by the authorities.

How long does it require to clear imported cargo thru the bureau of customs? At least a month or probably more, even if all papers are in order. Why not discharge the cargo directly from the boat crane into the waiting truck of the consignee's broker? After loading the truck, this goes to the clearing section, the boxes opened, examined, and appraised by a team of customs men, the declared duty paid right there and then by the consignee to the waiting customs cashier. The whole process should not take more than a few hours. More cargoes will be cleared at the least time, and more customs duties will be paid to the government.

Have the bureaucrats never heard of Henry Ford, the great genius of mass production by means of which he reduced the price of the automobile to within reach of the average American, and was responsible for paying the highest wages in the industry? All these Henry Ford accomplished through his original and creative idea of the assembly line method, the great legacy he left for the benefit of mankind. Let this be installed figuratively or literally in every government bureau and office having to do with the public waiting to be served to pay his taxes, prosecute a license, or to follow up some paper or document for approval. Let all office desks be so arranged as to permit a logical and continuous flow of papers from one desk to another until the document is finally approved by all concerned at the quickest time possible. Only then may Mr. Juan Publico sigh with relief, "Ah! this government means business!" Sometime ago, I applied for a loan from my insurance company. After filling in the application form which was examined by the processing clerk and found to be in order I was asked to wait. "May I come for the check tomorrow?" I asked. "Why tomorrow?" said the clerk. "Because I may have to wait long and I need to go back to my office." "Can you not wait for twenty minutes?" "Is that possible in twenty minutes?" I exclaimed. "You may even get your check probably in 15 minutes." So, I stayed and waited and in 15 minutes on the dot I got my loan-check. If such efficiency in a private company is possible, I just wonder why the same degree of efficiency is not possible in a government office. Try the ordeal of paying something to the government. Compare the same procedure of paying to a private firm and see the difference.

Revamp the police system

Thirdly, I would suggest the complete revamp of the police system of the country in order that our people should have more respect of the law, for civic order, and for decency. The great late Manila Mayor Lacson conceived that for people to respect the law, the city should have respectable policemen. And he thought that the more respect for the policeman could be gotten if the policemen were respectable college graduates. I would suggest that a police commission be formed in every town and city in this country. The commission shall consist of the municipal judge, the Catholic priest, the Protestant minister, the president of the Jaycees, and the president of the Rotary Club, and a few other leading citizens but no politician. The commission, to be headed by the Police Commissioner, shall have the power to recruit from the town's top college graduates of the current year to undertake two years of compulsory duty in the police force, in lieu of military duty. The recruitment shall be staggered in such a way that a proper portion of the police force is composed of seniors, juniors, and plebes for reasons which are quite obvious. Eventually, after sometime, the whole police force would be composed of college graduates, some of them from the cream of university graduates who will be exposed and thereby become sensitive to the problems of their community and will gain firsthand knowledge of these problems. Being a member of the elite of the town or community, his father, brothers and close relatives will be virtually members of an unofficial junior police team to lend a helping hand and moral support to their boy who is doing his civic duty for his community.

Population Program

Next, I would suggest that the government now make a

declared policy to stabilize population growth. Let all doctors and nurses of the bureau of health, and the social workers, all puericulture centers undertake the education of mothers and fathers on the accepted methods of birth control, as approved generally, based on our religion and tradition.

According to the statistics of the national economic council, the increase of the gross national product of the country over the years starting from liberation to the present time is steady. In fact, the slope of the gross national product increase is admirable when compared to that of other developing countries similar to the Philippines. Sad to say, however, the gross national product per capita over the years from liberation to the present time is almost a straight line showing no perceptible tendency to rise. In fact it is observed that in some years it has a tendency to dip. Since the gross national product per capita is the yardstick of the standard of living of our country, this conclusion is inescapable: Our standard of living is not getting any better from liberation to the present time. This means paradoxical when we know that a thousand factories have mushroomed in the suburbs of Manila. We have started to mechanize our agriculture, fertilize and irrigate our farms. Another conclusion also seems inescapable: that the rise in population growth has been too steep in proportion to our production, so much so that the quotient of G.N.P. divided by the number of people in any given year is almost stagnant. This is a sad commentary: "In our country the rich get richer while the poor get more children." Our standard of living is one of the lowest in the world, and because of the present conditions obtaining this low standard of living has not improved at all.

As a corollary, capital formation in this country comes at a very slow pace. This is so because the average family does not have the extra money to buy insurance, to deposit in a savings bank, or to buy stocks and bonds of industrial corporations which are the money pools on which industry depends to finance her enterprises. That the average family cannot buy insurance, deposit savings in a bank, buy stocks and bonds is obvious because it earns just enough or barely enough to feed and maintain its numerous members.

A former President of this country had dramatically stated that next to the problem of improving the standard of living of the Filipino, the greatest problem is how to stabilize our population growth. That was said many years ago. Nothing, nothing at all was done to implement the wisely pronounced policy.

In advocating family planning for our people let it be understood by all and sundry that we should not forget to strive to increase our production. By all means let us forever endeavor to increase our production -double it, triple it, increase it ten-fold.

However, simultaneously, let us also strive to stabilize our explosive population growth and we will begin to realize what is quite obvious: an increase G.N.P. divided by a stabilized population equals a quotient which will be reasonably increased.

Conservation

My next suggestion can be aptly called conservation. Specifically the leadership in our government should make it a pronounced national policy to conserve our resources and economize in our expenses, whether in the government sector or in the private sector. To cite an example: At one time the machinery firm for whom I work as an engineer was consulted by a big club in Manila on how to reduce its enormous water bill and improve its water supply system. After installing the Nawasa-recommended underground water reservoir into the club's pipelines, we inspected and repaired every faucet, valve, water closet and water fixture of the club in such a way that almost no single drop of water is wasted. The net result was that the water bill was reduced to less than ¼ the original amount. That was verified by the Nawasa engineers and auditors who were at first surprised at the drastic economy effected, but who later remarked that if the whole city of Manila and suburbs -all public buildings and private homes and residences and factories were to repair all leaky valves and faucets there will be no water shortage for Greater Manila. We should be taught a healthy respect for water, that sparkling clean water provided by the Nawasa comes out of an expensive and complicated system of filtering, aerating, washing, chlorinating, etc. We should not take water for granted just as we cannot take the fishes in our seas and the timber in our forests for granted; and yet our fishermen do not seem to respect our fishes. They catch the small fishes without giving them the chance to grow up so that we may derive the maximum benefit thereof. They catch the fish even during the mating season; not only that; they dynamite the fish, poison the fish, electrocute the fish and even use the carbonated soft drink to explode in a school of fish. It is my understanding that in other countries certain fishes of less than the legal length is returned to the sea. The same charge of wastefulness can also be leveled against the kaingeros and the unscrupulous lumber men who ravage our forests.

A great senator of the Philippines admonished us to avoid excessive food during fiestas. Let us also learn to finish our plates during parties and get only the amount of food that we can completely finish. It is a sad commentary that with some people their eyes are bigger than their stomachs. According to Seneca, "economy is in itself a source of great revenue."

Teachers

Of pressing necessity at this time is the solution of the problem to up-grade the quality of our teachers. Why are we producing half-baked college graduates? Why does a small percentage of the candidates that take the government board examinations manage to pass? It is said that a chain is no longer strong than its weakest link. The caliber of our high school and college graduates cannot be better than the caliber of our teachers and professors. Observe an average high school graduating class. Most of the upper third pursue studies in medicine, engineering, law; only a very few take up education. Most of the high school graduates that pursue studies in education do not belong to the upper third bracket. This is altogether paradoxical. As a wit quipped, "When a doctor makes a mistake, he buries it; when an architect makes a mistake, he covers it with ivy; but when a teacher makes a mistake, he may become a member of the School Board." It is in the teaching profession that we cannot afford the luxury of making a mistake because the mistake is necessarily perpetuated. Why don't we devise a system to rigidly screen our would-be teachers so that only he ablest may be allowed to teach? Why not motivate our ablest talents to donate a few hours a week of teaching our young? I am sure many able men and women will answer the challenge.

Dignify the lowly Filipino.

Then lastly, but only in this Preface, is my suggestion that the government leadership take positive steps to recognize and dignify the lowly Filipino. It was that great Filipino nationalist and patriot, Dr. Jose P. Laurel, who said that the common denominator in human relations is recognition and dignification of the human personality. In our society, where the prevailing modus Vivendi is unahan (cutting in line), gulangan (coercive cheating), and lamangan (bullying and brute force), the average Filipino is far from recognized and dignified as a human being. The great dean of a famous graduate school in the Philippines has been forever admonishing our leadership to exert efforts to alleviate the plight of our working man whose living conditions are so abject and so substandard, it is a wonder how he and his family can manage to keep body and soul together. This is the family that lives in a hovel --probably a rented first floor or a dilapidated house in a muddy neighborhood, or perhaps in a shanty, squatting in somebody's land. He earns a few pesos a day, sometimes, which is barely enough to feed himself and his family. This is the family that the puericulture center and the social worker should teach family planning. This is the family that deserves the greatest attention and solicitude of the social welfare department of our government. This is the family for whom I speak of conservation and economy in our government in order that the extra money saved may be spent for their welfare. This is the family for whom the government must build more and more low cost tenements so that they may have life a little bit more decently. This is the family which inspired our great President Magsaysay to say, "He who has less in life should have more in law."

Fantasy

There are several more suggestions that will come in this book or novelette. Because of the natural adverse reaction of people to suggested changes, this book was written as a sort of fantasy. It tells the story of a man (Juanito) who left his country to work abroad, ostensibly to earn more money the better to support to support his family but actually he left in disgust over the sad state of affairs of the country being badly run by the unscrupulous politicians and cynical attitude of the people in or outside the government. On pain of being likened to the class prophet delivering the class prophesy, the changes for the better are fait accompli. Let me point out that this man (Juanito) who returned to his country may be someone who had not actually left the country physically. He may be someone who perhaps had turned cynical about the sad affairs around him, about which he feels he cannot do anything because the problems appear too big for him to solve, and resignedly and conveniently hibernated into the peace and quiet of his cozy little world, ala Rip Van Winkle. Remember your graduation day in high school? Now listen to this fantastic class prophesy.

Chapter 1 - Coming Home

And the weather was just fine for coming home. Indeed it was almost perfect for him. He had expected the tropical air too warm for him who had known mild weather, but it was just right as he felt it envelope him when he went down the airplane's ramp. A slight breeze was blowing, and after making a mental note of the directions, he at once surmised that it must have come from the bay just a kilometer or so away. And the breeze wafted the smell of home. Yes, home. Home which he had not known for exactly fifteen years to the day.

Juanito Esguerra left home fifteen years ago on the pretext of searching for greener pastures in other lands. He had lied to his friends and relatives, told them that insofar as he was concerned his country could offer no more opportunities that he could successfully exploit to the fullest. He was not unsuccessful in his profession, and he could be pointed to as the man who had made first base. It was therefore not difficult for his friends to believe his lie.

But his more discerning relatives and friends of course saw through the lie. It was quite evident that there were other reasons, far better ones, for his departure, and his friends felt so. They didn't exactly know what those reasons were, and they won't dare ask. Nor would they try to read his mind or his heart.

At the time he left the country he was a very frustrated and heartbroken man. He had visions of changing the times and the mores without simply crying, "O Tempora! O Mores." ("Oh, the times! Oh, the manners!"-Cicero or Shakespeare). He wanted change in the sad state of affairs of his country, change that would modify if not obliterate the cynicism building up in the thinking of his countrymen then. If the country at the time were a turbulent sea, he offered himself as the slick of oil hat would help appease it. He tried to and tried as hard as the man who would be very pleased to see his hand stretched out to help, but he was frustrated by the seeming callousness that met his offer. He felt lost and bewildered as his attempts to sow the seeds of his ideas in the minds of his people are thwarted one after the other. Situations at the time seemed to have conspired and worked against him, militated against his ideas, shattered his heart and nearly broke his spirit.

And he had to go. He had to find a way out; not to escape, but to stave off a cruel thrust, to parry an attack which might prove fatal, to back pedal and in the process gain vigor so he could come back stronger. That was the tactic in his plan, the strategic withdrawal. He would lick his wounds, let them heal, and return. How long it would take him, how soon would he be able to return, he didn't know.

He was deep in thought when he suddenly heard a voice shatter the air calling his name.

"Welcome home, Father," it was his son calling.

"Juaning!" he exclaimed as his son approached and embraced him. He gave his son the once over, noted how much alike they were from head to foot.

"Well, well," he said. "Am I looking through a glass clearly? Why, we almost look alike. That forehead, that folksy face, that girth."

"But of course," said Juaning. "I am not your son for nothing. I was born unto your image."

He had named his son after him notwithstanding the objections that a son who is named after his father often become brother to the devil. He loved his son so much that he had wanted the boy to take after him. So he gave him his name and went out of his way to form him unto his image. And he was not disappointed. The boy lived up to his expectations.

His son was only a grade school tot when he decided to

leave the country. Unlike other boys of his age, however, his son showed an early precocity. It seemed then that he was old for his age. Conscientious, high minded, trustworthy and straightforward, the boy demonstrated admirable traits proving that could always be depended upon at all times.

He remembered very well how his son had wanted to go along with him and join him on his trip. He had to devise ways and means to dissuade the little tyke from becoming insistent, but it was only when he took him for a long man to man talk that the boy relented.

"Juaning," he told the boy then. "It may take me long before I could return to our country. In the meantime, someone has to take care of your mother. You are the only fellow upon whom I could depend. Nobody else could take care of your mother. So I hope you won't seriously take your going along with me."

There were moments of silence. Tears were welling in the boy's eyes. Before the boy could cry his heart out, he pursued his line.

"Your mother would be alone," he told his son. "You must stay and take good care of her."

Perhaps the admonition made a man out of the boy, because he no longer evinced any interest in going with his father.

Juaning corresponded with him constantly. The boy was an articulate correspondent and it was through him that he received first hand information about the conditions obtaining in the country as the years passed by. In the latter years they exchanged views on sundry topics to the ultimate satisfaction of both of them.

It was Juaning who rekindled the old fire in him. It was the son, the boy to whom he lent his name, who helped him much in assuaging his heart, in making his wounds heal. Gradually the affection which he had lost of his country and his people was restored. Little by little his fondness returned, especially when Juaning wrote him of the changes that were being made in the country.

"I could not exactly describe the changes that are being made in our country today." Juaning had written in one of his letters. "They are beyond words. You have to see them with your eyes, feel them yourself, to believe them."

In almost every letter that Juaning penned him, there was always the plea for him to come home. The boy's letters kept drumming into his ears the refrain, "Come home! Come home!" Somehow something had to give, and he gave in to his son's pleas. He had to come home.

(Recall 1a)
On the plane taking him home he found the time to

cogitate on Juaning's statement that a tremendous change had been made in the country. The causes of this change had intrigued him endlessly. What could have made it? What wrought the change? Was there an upheaval? What made the change?

He was quietly speculating on the matter when it occurred to him that many years back he had brought forth a thesis on education for harmonious relations. Could it be that the ideas he had integrated in his thesis had finally taken root in the country?

Harmonious Human Relations (HHR), as he had defined it, is the ability to get along with people. It is the unknown in the human equation that has to be satisfied. Implanted and developed in a man's personality, H.H.R., as he wanted the subject to be known, it could work wonders.

He had chosen to name the subject H.H.R. for several reasons. First, he didn't want the subject to sound too idealistic or moralistic if he labels it "Character Education", although it would really teach character education. Because of this possibility, it would naturally draw fire from the cynics and the skeptics. He wanted a name that would be acceptable to the average man, to the man on the street. Second, he wanted a name that would be indicative of the happy philosophy of mutual convenience between "me and the other fellow." He could have named it "Education for Community Living" which would have been equally fitting, but he finally chose "Education for Harmonious Human Relations" or HHR, for short.

He conceived of the idea of developing the thesis "Education for Harmonious Human Relations" after carefully weighing the fast events at the time which led him to conclude that there was an urgent need for studying the art of human relations. Powerful nations at the time seemed to be bracing for the Armageddon, the war to end all wars, and this was evident in their mad contest as to who would be the first to produce the most powerful bomb, who would be the first in space, and who would be first in the moon. In fact there was a cold war that was slowly but surely threatening to turn hot at the slight squeeze of the trigger. East was pitted against West, color pitted against color, nation against nation, brother against brother.

In the mad competition nations were appropriating a greater bulk of their incomes in developing weapons of war, armies, navies and air forces. Spy networks operating on a world wide scale were also getting a good portion of the national incomes just so one nation could protect itself from another or take over the realm of another. It was a waste, indeed a great waste for nations to be pursuing such aims at the sacrifice of far better things. They could use the monies they were spending for arms and for arming themselves for other purposes, like investing them towards the improvement of the human race. The world would be a better place to live in if the money that was just going down the drain for so-called defense appropriations were used in the building of homes, the production of better home appliances, the construction of schools, hospitals, libraries and gymnasiums.

But of course there was a reason for all this madness. There was at the time mutual fear among nations, especially the powerful ones. There existed mutual fear among men. People distrusted each other. One was always on his guard because the other might put one over him.

How to erase this eroding thought from the minds of men became the issue of the day, the issue which he proposed to be met with the study of the art of human relations. He believed then, as he believes now, that a person who had undertaken the art of human relations would ultimately resolve the conflict between men due to such reasons as politics, economics, religion, geography or ideology. There would be no wars in this world which in all is recorded history has known only 14 years of complete peace, according to a well known historian.

Gaining knowledge in the art of human relations could be achieved through the teaching of the subject, "Education For Harmonious Human Relations," a subject so dear to his heart. It is a subject that could easily, effectively, forcefully and interestingly taught even to grade schoolers. In fact, in his thesis he wanted it taught in the fourth grade of elementary education through high school to the Humanities of the Liberal Arts in college. A compendium of do's and don'ts, or specific acts and omissions in man's daily life, harmonious human relations could be taught without difficulty because it would purposely omit generalities and principles which were easy to forget. The possibility that the importance of the subject might not be able to catch on the individual could be solved by extending the promotion of the subject in public offices, libraries, gymnasiums and buses by means of posters and notices; in cinemas by means of trailers, documentaries or slides; in churches through the help of the men of the cloth.

Just what are the specific acts and omissions that should be taught? He had observed that there were indeed only a few specific acts and omissions that could be taught in order to start the ball rolling. The list would be surprisingly short, because as the list grows it would be noted that some specific acts and omissions constitute the realm of good manners and citizenship training and bordering on the area of harmonious human relations. In fact these subjects closely overlap each other to a great extent that they are all synonymous.

Top among the few specific and particular acts and omissions that would constitute harmonious human relations was how to spit or blow one's nose in public. Most people spit or blow their noses without attempting to consider the next fellow, thus inconveniencing the latter with his saliva or mucus spray. This is the wrong way. The correct way in doing it is to spit or blow one's nose into a handkerchief or a piece of tissue paper which should later be thrown into a trash can. Or, if one neither has hanky or piece of tissue paper, one should squat first then spit or blow his nose into the gutter. Or, if it is possible, one should refrain from spitting or blowing one's nose in public.

Another specific act is the manner of smoking in the street or in a public conveyance. A smoker walking in a crowded street who holds his cigarette in the conventional way may in more ways than one harm other people by burning another fellow's arm or burn another's apparel. Or, a careless smoker riding in a bus or jeepney may cause the flying embers from his cigarette to hurt the other fellow's eyes or burn his clothes. These are the ways that should be corrected. A considerate smoker cups his hand over the lighted end of his cigarette while walking in the street or riding in a public conveyance. This way he could avoid a lot of unpleasantness.

Most people never give a thought on how they should comport themselves while riding in a public conveyance. One passenger, for instance, occupies more than his rightful share of the bus or jeepney seat. Or he sprawls his feet in the aisle causing inconvenience to other passengers. Or he places a package or bundle on the seat preventing other passengers from sitting conveniently. Or he places his umbrella or basket in the aisle. All these are the ways of rude persons who would rather see their fellowmen squirming in discomfiture than yield an inch in the name of good breeding. This could be corrected if people only bear in mind that upon boarding a bus hey should proceed to the farthest end of the seat, one that is not near the door and occupy only their rightful share of the seat. If they carry packages, they should put them on their lap. They should put their feet under the seat as far inside as possible. If they have an umbrella they should put it out of the way of other passengers.

These are only a few of the specific acts and omissions that should be taught. Stripped of their trimmings, these specific acts and omissions point out that people should be considerate of others. In other words, they should not be utterly selfish. They should give a little of themselves to others. The smoker who hurts another with his carelessness should realize that he may one day be on the lighted cigarette end of another. The thoughtless passenger who hogs his seat or sprawls his feet should also consider how he would feel if he were the one who was being inconvenienced.

The subject really would not be difficult to teach, providing the instruction should be carried out in a practical down-to-earth manner and not in the idealistic, moralistic, dogmatic, holier-than thou vein. It was his contention that man does not really demand from his fellowmen much more than the equitable share of convenience in order to live and let live. All he really needs is equity. All he wants is to strike at the golden mean or express the happy-medium philosophy of mutual convenience between "me and the other fellow."

He had high hopes that his thesis would be accepted because he believed in what Dr. Joshua L. Liebman, a great preacher and writer, had once said: "People are the great mines filled with rich ore, waiting to be discovered and brought to the surface of the earth." He also wanted to echo the words of Prof. Eduard C. Lindeman, renowned editor and educator, who said: "An organism becomes what it does. A person's character takes on the pattern of his acts, not is wishes. We become what we do."

(Recall 1b)

Creating a good idea is one, and sharing it with others is another. He knew too well that he had created a good idea and he wanted to share it with others. In the words of Lowell Fillmore: "A good idea that is not shared with others will gradually fade away and bear no fruit, but when it is shared it lives forever, because it is passed from one person to another as it goes." If he had profited from its beneficence, he wanted others to profit from it too. He was that unselfish, so he took no time in putting down his ideas on paper which would later shape into the thesis that was dear to his heart. Then he beat the path leading to the educational pundits of the land.

He was bubbling with great expectations when he broached the idea of the introduction into the school curriculum of the subject: "Education for Harmonious Human Relations." He expounded on his thesis as if he was defending it in a "revalida" ("masters final oral exam"). They listened briefly and stopped at it. They didn't even bother to scratch the surface of the matter to look if it was gold or dross that was being offered to them.

If that was frustrating, what followed was heart-breaking because it took the form of seemingly outright dismissal. The educational pundits, or that was what they wanted to be known, argued that the teaching of human relations in school was unnecessary.

Human relations, which he had proposed to teach under the subject, "Education for Harmonious Human Relations" is common sense, said the educators. It is already covered by our Civil, Penal, Mercantile, and other codes. People already have religion. "People are like rough pebbles thrown into the revolving drum of life. Their rough edges will eventually smoothened" (from a famous saying).

Human relations should be taught by parents. It is too

complicated to be included in the school curriculum. Its teaching would be tantamount to regimentation. It is a big order.

But of course, it is a big order. It is a big order because it would completely revamp the whole setup and rejuvenate the morals of our people.

Is human relations common sense? He had asked himself then. It was giving credit indeed, to the average man, and this can be considered dangerous. Quoting Clinton F. Carlson, former Grand Master of Philippine Masons, he said in arguing his point: "Good manners are logical and make sense perfectly. Yet, there are people who are unconsciously boorish, who could not possibly display good manners because of faulty background. There are people who could not react to the spirit of lofty ethics, people who do not know that such spirit exists. All around us are men and women prevented by limitations or rearing, of mentality, of temperament, of experience, from acting to the canons of behavior."

No, human relations is not common sense. It is uncommon sense that should be developed in a man. It is a thing that should be cultivated, taught, learned to prepare one's mental habits. One may have the potential but if it is not properly developed it becomes useless. It must be experienced, otherwise it loses its impact.

And what if human relations is covered by our code of laws? Most of us die without knowing what a code of law looks like. Moreover, lawyers could be living example of who may know the codes of law but who do not know a whit about human relations. Man may manage to live within the pale of the law and yet commit what is known as man's inhumanity to man. Although there is really a relation between human relations and the law, yet there exists a gap between the lines of the law that needs filling in by the art of human relations in order to make life in the community tolerable for the inhabitants.

Although religion has a bearing on human relations, it is not a determinant in the art of human relations. A man may have religion, may be steeped in religion, but it does not give him a clean bill of health insofar as getting along with others is concerned.

Are people comparable to rough pebbles which when thrown into the revolving drum of life eventually get smoothened? The question is moot. There are people who learn and there are people who could learn but would not learn. In other words, people do not necessarily become smoothened eventually because they have been thrown into the revolving drum of life. Granting without admitting that the smoothening would eventually come, but why then wait or a long time? Why not start early? Why not pre-polish them in the art of human relations before throwing them into the revolving drum of life? To resort to another analogy, how can we proceed to clean the waters of a swimming pool with new water? We cannot change the population of this country with a new breed overnight. The dirty water of a swimming pool is filtered gradually, constantly: the degree of cleanliness of the water is gradually and constantly increased.

It is the duty of parents to teach their children human relations, so the educational pundits argued. How could parents teach without knowing what they are going to teach? It would be a case of a blind man leading the blind. Young people imbibing from their teachers the knowledge of human relations could teach their parents in the art.

The educational pundits also argued that human relations would be too complicated to include in the school curriculum. But he believed that there would be no complication at all. On the contrary, if one would list the specific and particular acts and omissions that constitute good human relations, he would find the list very short. In fact, it would be necessary to consolidate human relations with such allied subjects as Good Manners, Character Education, Citizenship Training and other related subject to constitute a full subject entitled "Human Relations" because these subjects complement each other.

The argument that the teaching of Human Relation would be tantamount to regimentation was rather off the mark. Is asking motor vehicles to take the right side of the road or pedestrians to walk along pedestrian lanes regimentation? Is the prohibition of smoking inside a movie house when a city ordinance expressly prohibits it regimentation? Is asking people to obey the law regimentation? Teaching certain specific and particular acts and omissions to attain harmony when man is in contact with his fellowmen is not regimentation. According to J.H. McPherson, "conformity in behavior is a human necessity; it is conformity in patterns of thought which is a human danger."

Yes, teaching Human Relations in the school is a big order. It is a big order in the sense that it would herald the change in this world. But it is not a big order because it would be difficult to each. Hardly any Filipino knew how to speak and write English when the Americans came in 1898, but by 1930 English was already the official language of the country. This was made possible by the inclusion of English in the school curriculum. This could also be done with respect to human relations. If a totally foreign tongue could be successfully taught to a people in 30 years, it can be expected that better success would meet the teaching of the livelier and more interesting subject of human relations.

(Recall 1c)

His was a voice in the wilderness. Nobody heard him. He shouted hard and nobody heard. He felt low. Everything around him looked dark. He winced every time he saw people demonstrating their lack of education in the fine art of human relations. How it broke his heart to think that they could have profited well from his thesis were it not for the narrow-mindedness of the educational pundits (so-called) in the land. His country could have been the first in the world to deliberately develop **geniuses in the art of human relations.**

He recalled vividly the central idea of his thesis:

We speak of geniuses in the arts and sciences, such as a musical genius, a literary genius, a genius in mathematics. We speak also of geniuses in technology and industry, such as mechanical genius, an electrical wizard, a genius in mass production, etc., and yet we have never heard of geniuses in the art of human relations.

Is this because we are totally unaware that there is such a person who is a genius in human relations? Or it is believed there exists no such genius in the art of human relations? Or because it is not considered possible to develop a person to become a genius in the art of human relations? If so, then it is high time for us to set our sights higher and to try to develop geniuses in the art of human relations. How?

We learn that one of the most important elements, if not the most important, in genius, is the ability to derive the general law from the particular, which is also called generalization, or induction --the passage from instance to law. Only a genius can do this. The opposite of this process, the derivation of the particular from the general, is called deduction, which ordinary people can do. Of course, there are other elements in the making of a genius, such as: oneness of purpose, concentration, tenacity, and perseverance, industry, creativeness. But of these elements, the ability of induction is generally considered the most important.

Then by all means, let the student of human relations be taught only specific and particular acts and omissions which constitute harmonious human relations and purposely omit teaching any generalities or principles, and afford the student the golden opportunity to discover for himself and by himself the general law of human relations from the particular and specific acts that were taught to him and actually practiced by him. This discovery by the student may be a slow and gradual process, like the dawning of the morning sun. Or this discovery may be instantaneous, like the gleam of light which flashes across his mind from within, for which Emerson has been forever teaching us to be on the lookout.

What the student will discover as a general law may be the so-called Golden Rule which is the basic tenet of most religions; or he may discover that the general law is "humanity's commonness" or "togetherness" as termed by the Family of Man show; or he may discover that is what pacifist organization calls "co-existence"; or he may discover that it is what Dr. Jose P. Laurel aptly calls "Recognition and Dignificationn" of the human personality; or he may discover that it is what the United Nations call "Peace and Understanding"; or he may discover that it is what he YMCA calls "Fellowship". Let the student call it anything from his point of view and personal circumstances, because he will find out that human relations is "many splendor thing", just as there may be only one truth but it has a thousand facets. But our main concern is to guide the student to undertake the so-called "inductive leap" and thereby discover the general law by himself and for himself. Then we would have succeeded in preparing the student to become a genius or near-genius in the art of human relations. Need we ask for more?

Aided by this "mental hygiene" of practicing the selected specific acts and omissions that constitute harmonious human relations, ever believing even without actually attaining the "perfectibility of mankind", man can attain the stature of the truly "evolved man", cleansed and immune from his past plagues of actual wars and chronic disputes.

Inspired men have said again and again that what man can do is almost limitless. A famous scientist once said: "Anything the human mind can conceive can be accomplished." Unfortunately most people interpret this only in terms of material things like visual telephones, pocket-sized two-way radios, interplanetary ships, etc. May not a portion of man's limitless capacity to achieve anything be properly channeled and dedicated to improve human relations? Nature is on our side to help us improve our human relations. Man is said to be created by God in His image, and he was born good and pure. According to Dr. Benito F. Reyes, the greatest Filipino philosopher today, "God considered Man the most beloved of all his creations --into who else's nostrils did God breath a soul?" God in his infinite wisdom allowed no baby to come out of his mother's womb already bad. Much of the so-called man's inhumanity to man is unintentional. That the average man may not know how to live in harmony with his fellowmen is only so because he was not taught any better. There is hardly anything in the rough edges of man's character which cannot be smoothened by the proper study of the art of human relations.

According to the late Bernard Baruch, one of the world's greatest elder statesmen: "We cannot cast out pain from the world, but needless suffering we can. Tragedy will be with us in some degree as long as there is life, but misery we can banish. Injustice will raise its head in the best of all possible worlds, but tyranny we can conquer. Evil will invade some men's hearts, intolerance will twist some men's minds, but decency is a far more common human attribute and it can be made to prevail in our daily lives."

"I believe all his because I believe above all else in reason --in the power of the human mind to cope with the problems of life. To do nothing so much as the abandonment of reason does humanity owe its sorrows. Whatever failures I have known, whatever errors I have committed, whatever follies I have witnessed in private and public life have been the consequences of action without thought."

Let us now call on Carl Gustav Jung, one of our greatest psychologists: "I am convinced that the study of the soul is the science of the future. It becomes increasingly evident that neither famine, nor earthquakes, nor microbes, nor cancer, but man, is the greatest danger to man, and this for the reasons that we have no sufficient protection against psychotic epidemics, which can work infinitely more destruction than the greatest catastrophe of nations. People must understand from what quarter danger was threatening them."

Next let us hear from Billy Graham, one of the greatest and most inspiring evangelists today: "Certainly we are nearer the day of reckoning in the development of the terrible hydrogen bombs. We have reached the point of no return. Unless human nature can be radically changed within the next few years, there is every possibility that these bombs will someday be unleashed upon the world."

Lastly, before I rest my case, allow me to quote my last witness, August J. Seiloff, American Grandmaster of Masons, who said: "The problem of learning how to live together on this world --all of us, everywhere is squarely upon us; we cannot dodge or defer it. In our time we must meet it. We either wipe out one another by science's fearsome weapons of destruction, or we learn to live together. It is simple as that."

May the Board of National Education of this country deem it fitting to include in the school curriculum the compulsory subject of Harmonious Human Relations. May the educational planners of other countries follow suit.

Although he felt bitter about it all, he did not show it in his countenance. His "big dream" to spark-plug the turning point in the solution of his country's pressing problems was shattered. He might be the same standing on his frame, but he was never the same man anymore. He had gone into battle and had been wounded. The wounds were festering into sores. It would need time to them heal. It would need a long time, long time indeed.

Chapter 2 - Changes For The Better

"How long have you been gone, father? Juaning asked as

they drove away from the airport.

"I don't know exactly," he said. "I haven't counted the years." He paused, then asked: "How old are you now?"

"Twenty-five on my last birthday," Juaning replied.

"You were only a strapping kid of ten when I left," he said. "Take away ten from twenty-five and you have the number of years that I had been away."

"Fifteen years," Juaning said. "That's a long time."

"Yes," he said. "A long time to be away from home."

"Mother could not come," Juaning said. "She said that if she went along with me there would be no one to prepare the house for your homecoming."

"She is the same woman I have known for many years," he said. "She used to tell me in the early years of our marriage that a wife's work could never end. She seems to be living up to the letter of the expression."

The car turned left on a short street and then turned right for the boulevard. It was early morning and the boulevard was swarming with cars all of which were running with the same speed. With the exception of a police car that passed them by with sirens wailing, nobody seemed interested in overtaking. He remembered that many years ago these same number of vehicles running in one area of the city would be more than enough to create chaos. It was easy to create bedlam. Just put five motor vehicles on the road whose drivers wouldn't know what was right and what was wrong, whose knowledge of the rules of the road cold be put on a pin head and you would have a traffic jam that would take hours to untangle.

He was beginning to wonder about the event that was unfolding before him when his eyes caught the car's speedometer. It registered 40. He noticed that the needle seem to move beyond 40 although it indicated a number below 40 when the car slowed down before they approached a busy corner. His curiosity was getting the better of him when he inquired from Juaning about the event that was transpiring before his eyes.

"Motor vehicles in our country do not go beyond 40, inside or outside towns and cities," Juaning said. "That's the law."

"The law?" he asked.

"Sort of," Juaning said. "You see, many years ago a President of our country finally realized that he should act with the diligence and care of a good father of the family, so he issued an executive order strictly limiting the speed of motor vehicles on our streets to 40 kilometers per hour. To make certain that the order would be followed to the letter, the President required the installation of speed governors in all motor vehicles, except police cars, ambulances, fire truck and army vehicles. Abstracts of this executive order were required to be posted inside all motor vehicles and in front of drivers. You see this sticker? That's an abstract of the executive order. Now no self-respecting motor vehicle driver guns his car to a speed of more than 40. The result was at the end of the year the number of deaths due to traffic accidents was almost nil, compared to former annual take-for granted average of about 700.

But he was not listening to his son anymore. His mind was again busy recalling the past years, particularly the time he wrote that one of the most deteriorating factor in human relations is speed, unreasonable speed, which he made to read as either so slow as to become a snail's pace, or so fast as to endanger life and limb. He expounded in his thesis that young people should be taught that if they ever drive a car they should do so within limits and in a manner that they would not be able to splash water or raise dust as the case may be, on pedestrians and houses bordering the street.

He was, however, quite particular with the effect of speed on the man on the street. He had decried the fact that most of the country's streets had been so constructed as if the motor vehicle was more important than the pedestrian. It was a supreme insult on man whom God had made to walk erect, head high and arms swinging. How could man do so in most streets? The absence of pedestrian lanes and sidewalks coupled with the unreasonable speed that motor vehicles were driven, how could man maintain his dignity?

Driving at an unreasonable speeds, to his mind, was cruel, sadistic, inhuman, fiendish, not to say wasteful and improvident. Cruel because it impose great pain on other people; sadistic because only men with warped minds would do it; inhuman because no man in his right mind would drive at an unreasonable speeds; and fiendish because it makes no exception. It is wasteful and improvident, for it accounts for a great part of the economic losses that the country suffers.

Speeding on the highways had caused so much loss to life and limb. In the United States alone, statistics show that the total number of Americans killed in traffic accidents is greater than the total number killed in all the wars the US had fought from the war of independence to world war II. The toll in this country was also high and getting higher every year. Considering that the country had narrow highways and streets, there is no gainsaying that more accidents are happening each day. One has only to take into consideration the fact if airplanes collide in the limitless skies and ships ram each other in the wide expanses of our oceans, how much more would it be likely for two motor vehicles running at unreasonable speeds on our narrow highways to collide.

If motorists would have only sense to run their vehicles at reasonable speeds then, they would be able to contribute much to the economic welfare of the country. Unfortunately most of our motorists are either stupid or do not know any better. By running their motor vehicles at unreasonable speeds they unwittingly run themselves into an expensive proposition. They just don't know that the wear and tear their motor vehicles suffer because of the unreasonable speed at which they run them, the wear and tear which roads and highways suffer, not to mention the greater cost of fuel they pay for indulging their folly, all add up to an expense that is quite staggering. In fact the loss which the nation suffers because of high speeds of motor vehicles is terrific.

Speeding motorists should also realize that they cause a lot of people untold sufferings. The dust that they raise while going at fast clips bring pulmonary diseases. The mud that they splash on people and the nerves that they shatter create situations that are uncomplimentary.

Taking into account all these things that are caused by motorists who run their vehicles at unreasonable speeds, and equating them to money, anybody who can do simple arithmetic would arrive at an amount that would have gone to projects that would spell economic prosperity.

In the face of wantonness with which certain motorists treat the subject of speeding on our highways, everything seemed hopeless. But as the saying goes, hope springs eternal, and to every problem there must always be a solution, possibly an elegant solution.

It was in this spirit that he had grappled with the problem of unreasonable speed at which motorists run on roads, streets and highways. The solution he had proffered in his thesis was education for harmonious human relations, or HHR and a speed governor.

He had in HHR the specific act of regulating the speed of motor vehicles. He recalled coining the term, "moral speed" of motor vehicles which connotes a deeper meaning than legal speed. Motor vehicle speeds must be regulated to the satisfaction of all. It is common knowledge that motor vehicles which run too slow cause so much chagrin as motor vehicles that run too fast. Hence, he had proposed that motor vehicles, with the exception of police cars, ambulances, fire trucks and army vehicles, be run at not over 40 kph. This speed is quite reasonable considering that a motor vehicle at this peed goes at least ten times faster than a pedestrian. Tests have also proven that if two motor vehicles at the speed of 40 kph collide head-on, their passengers would not run the risk of being severely injured.

But his pet solution was the installation of a speed governor in the motor vehicle. A speed governor could do a lot of wonders. In the first place no one would be tempted to run his motor vehicle more than the allowed rate of speed because of the speed governor. In other words there would be no undue speeding.

"Daydreaming, father?" he heard Juaning said.

"No," he replied. "I was just comparing past events with what I am now seeing."

"So you noticed the change," Juaning aid. "It is only one of the many changes that I have been telling you in my letters. There are many others. Did you notice the proper parking of cars and that there is absolutely no double parking? In fact, if I may be allowed to exaggerate a little, you have come home to an entirely changed country."

Juaning cut their conversation short when he saw the traffic signal   at   the   intersection.

Chapter 3 -The Policeman

Juaning eased the car as they came to an intersection where a policeman was directing traffic. Juanito saw the policeman raise a white-gloved hand to make a stop signal, which Juaning failed to see immediately. When he finally saw it, it was a little too late that he had to kick at the brakes. Suddenly Juaning felt ill at ease, knowing that he had committed a mistake and expecting the policeman to approach him momentarily.

The policeman saw to it that the traffic was orderly when he left his post and walked towards the Esguerra's car. A few steps from the car the policeman made a snappy salute at Juaning. When he neared the car he asked:

"Anything wrong, sir?" the policeman politely asked.

"Nothing serious," replied Juaning. "Just missed a cue."

"Are you sure everything's all right?" the policeman further inquired.

"Yes," said Juaning. "I m sure."

"Well, then, Sir," said the policeman. "I believe you don't need my services."

"No, thank you," said Juaning.

The policeman again made a snappy salute, executed about face smartly and returned to his post.

All the while Juanito Esguerra watched the little drama with mouth agape. He was as much amazed at the politeness of the policeman as he was proud at the way his son comported himself through it all. The policeman was a far cry from the policeman he had known in the past. The policeman he had seen was courteous, polite and refined, not to say articulate. The policemen he has generally known before he left the country were uncouth, uncivil and rugged. He was about to engage his son in a conversation about the

policeman when he caught the headline of a boxed story on the front page of the newspaper his son brought along. The headline read:
UP SUMMA CUM LAUDE HEADS POLICE TRAINEES.

The story below the headline read:
"Galileo Del Gallego, summa cum laude graduate of the University of the Philippines, heads this year's top graduates who will undertake compulsory police work as provided under the Police Act.

"Del Gallego took up engineering at the state university where he was a consistent scholar. He was awarded the UP president's pin for his high scholastic standing.

"Gen. Julio Espanto, commanding officer of the nation's top police training school, said that Del Gallego is the tenth summa cum laude graduate who will render compulsory police duty since the passage of the Police Act. The law drafting top college graduates to render police duty was enacted ten years ago."

Juanito Esguerra put down the newspaper and asked his son:

"What's this compulsory police duty?"

"Haven't you heard of it yet?" his son replied.

"No," he answered. "What's it all about?"

"I thought I wrote you about it when I was drafted to do police work after graduation from college."

"Maybe," he said. "But I didn't get the drift. Perhaps I was woolly that time. Receiving your letters then made me a bit woolly, you know."

"Well," he son exclaimed. "According to the law, the Police Act created in every town and city a police commission composed of the community's leading and respected citizens, which has the power to recruit from the town's top college graduates to undertake two-year police duty, in lieu of military service. Recruiting is staggered in such a way that half of the police force are "rookies" and the other half are "seniors". Making the top graduates render police duty has several purposes. Among others, the top college graduates add prestige to the policeman's calling. By rendering police duty for a certain period, these top graduates are able to gain the confidence of the people in our police agencies. They are also instrumental in giving police work a certain degree of dignity.

"According to the newspaper," he said, "this has been going on for the past ten years. What has it been able to do for the country in those ten years?"

"It has done the country a lot of good," Juaning said. " Take that policeman who approached us at the intersection where we made a sudden stop. He was polite and courteous. These traits in the policeman inspire confidence. Seeing these traits in people whom we had once known as rowdies, citizens no longer become afraid. You must remember that many years ago policemen were known to mulct you at the slightest mistake you make. In fact it was common for a peace-loving citizen to be held up by a policeman, so much so that the joke current then was that if a policeman approached you and did not hold you up, you were to immediately hie yourself to church to arrange that a mass be offered the next day thanking your ancestors.

"You must have also noticed that the policeman was sharp-eyed, otherwise he wouldn't have seen the car jerked when I applied the brakes. If he hadn't seen us, chances are that he was taking notes of what was transpiring before his eyes. What he has noted today might be what he had noted yesterday. In other words, nothing has happened yet that could be construed as a violation of the law while he was on duty because criminality in this city has already been minimized, if not thoroughly contained.

"Since the country's top graduates had rendered police duty," Juaning went on, "police agencies in the country changed a lot. Discipline had been instilled into the rank and file. You must have seen the snappy salutes of that policeman, his military bearing, and the smartness by which he had executed his steps. That is only part of his discipline.

"The crooks in the police departments had already been kicked out, the bad eggs had reformed. Although there are still instances of discipline breakdown, generally the picture of the policeman as a public servant has improved."

Juanito Esguerra remembered that before he left the country, the police agencies were in a bad state. Even Manila's Finest, the best police force in the country, was not spared the debilitating effects of the bad eggs and the crooks in the ranks. Extortionists, hold-uppers, rapists, maulers and assorted vermin that infested the underworld seemed to have just changed venues and move to the police ranks. Said a ranking P.C. officer: "Under the present system, anybody from the garbage can be appointed a policeman."

He remembered the case of the college basketball coach and the physician who were badly mauled by policemen, rookies at that. These two men were law-abiding citizens and deserved the protection of the police. But instead of getting the protection, they were instead given the works.

He also remembered the case of the lady professor who, after a rape attempt was made on her, was given a tough time by policemen. The case, given wide publicity by the newspapers, roused an indignant nation.

What he distinctly remembered, however, was the time his jeep was stolen which he reported by letter to the Mayor, the Police, the P.C. and the N.B.I. without benefit of even an acknowledgement. And he also remembered the time his niece's purse was snatched by a thief. His niece reported the matter to a policeman, but the policeman, instead of chasing the thief, had to investigate the poor girl. Then again there was the case of a friend whose apartment was burglarized. His friend reported the matter to the police by phone, expecting to get immediate help. His friend was shocked when he was told by the policeman on duty at the headquarters to report personally the matter, or get help somewhere else.

What was the country coming to? He had asked himself then. How did these policemen get to be what they were?

Decent citizens had been up in arms against the abuses of the police, but it seemed the authorities couldn't do anything about them. Investigations dragged on and more often than not ended up as whitewash affairs. The guilty were set free and made to prey on the poor helpless citizens again.

But good would overcome evil in the long run. If these people would only be run through the mill of his HHR, there would be great changes for the good, changes for the better.

If what he had seen and what Juaning had related to him was true, then changes must have been made in this country, he told himself. There must have been reforms that changed the face the nation.

If this is all true, he mused, the he could now call he policeman   on   the   beat   as   a   true   public   servant.

Chapter 4 - Public Servant

"It's a fine day, isn't it father? Juaning asked.

"Yes," he said. "It is a very fine day indeed."

He noticed the glow on Juaning's face. It emanated rays of happiness that touched him and made him happy, too. He knew that his son was very happy because he had come home, but he suspected that there was something more that made the boy happy. He was about to ask him why when Juaning spoke.

"You know, father, " Juaning said, pulling out a sheaf of papers from the glove compartment of the car. "I have just received an appointment from the government. Here are the appointment papers."

"This is very good news," he said, taking the papers. "Can I read them?"

"Yes, please," Juaning said.

He unfolded the papers and read.

DEPT OF PUBLIC WORKS & COMMUNICATIONS MANILA

January 2nd, 19xx

Mr. Juanito Esguerra, Jr. Pasay City, Philippines

Dear Mr. Esguerra,

You are hereby appointed Public Servant. Performing the duties of Electrical Engineer, with compensation at the rate of Seven Thousand Two Hundred Pesos per annum, effective upon taking oath.

As Public Servant, you are expected to perform your duties in accordance with the norm of conduct set forth by Sec. 1, Art III of the Revised Civil Service Act of 1959.

Very respectfully yours, MARIANO BATISTA Secretary

"I am happy you were extended the appointment of public servant," he said.

"I am happy too," Juaning said, "and yet sad."

"Why sad?" he asked

"You see," Juaning said, "when I was made to take my oath of office, I was required to bring my family. All I had was mother. How I wished you were around."

"Do you mean to say that the authorities would not let you take your oath of office if you didn't have your family around?" he asked.

"Yes," Juaning replied. "Your family is required to be around to add solemnity to an already solemn occasion."

"It was not done that way in the past," he said.

"That was in the past," Juaning said. "But things have already changed. They now believe your taking your oath of office with your family around makes you more responsible than if you were just handed the oath of office as if you were given a mere scrap of paper."

"You must have felt you were being inaugurated president of the country." he said.

"I was made to feel more than that, " Juaning replied.

"But why Public Servant?" he asked. He propounded the question although deep in his heart he knew why because many years ago he thought of just that.

"I believe emphasis was laid on 'public servant'," Juaning said, "because the mere mention of public servant in the appointment advances over the bureaucracy like a benign light over a benighted worker. Expected to be a catch phrase, it actually catches on so tenaciously that you are made to feel its effect everywhere."

"And it has produced a positive thinking in our people," Juaning continued. "It has produced a new breed that had locked horns in combat to the entrenched barnacles in the public service."

"And you know what?" Juaning said.

"What?"

"I memorized the acceptance of appointment by public servant which was made while taking the oath."

Juaning took a deep breath, then recited:

"In accepting the above appointment I solemnly and sincerely promise and swear that I will faithfully, honestly and with integrity serve as Public Servant performing the duties of Electrical Engineer. I am fully aware that the compensation I will receive as a public servant is the people's money; therefore, it is my bounden duty to serve the people with the fullest measure of devotion without mental reservation."

Again Juaning took a deep breath.

"Mother signed as a witness to that acceptance." Juaning said.

"Wonderful," Juanito said "Wonderful!"

(Recall 4a)

Again, **it was** time for him to muse as he pondered the words of his son. Time for him to make his thoughts soar.

There is wisdom in what my son had stated, he thought. It is wisdom born of necessity. People in the government, or people employed in enterprises selling services, should always bear in mind that they are in their jobs to perform a public service. They are there to be public servants. They are there to serve the people.

By public servant, of course, does not mean that the ordinary government employee should be beholden to the taxpayer that he would perform work expected only of menials. The matter should not be viewed in this perspective, because there is a great difference between services being rendered by a few for so many and the services of one for a compact few.

In other words, no one should have a misconception that because one is a public servant, one should perform the duties of a lackey, a bootlicker or anything near it. Being a public servant by its nature is the ability of one to perform services for the public good. It is not corruption of the word servant or a decline from the off-used word employee.

One who is a public servant possesses the most powerful instrument in doing greater service for the public good. It can be equated to the powers of a head of state.

Being called a public servant has many ramifications and one should prepare himself not to hear the last of it in the coming years.

People who get to be public servants should carry the title with honor. They should give the name its just compensation. Which reminds him of the government employee of old who had come to office in a white coat with upturned collar and in white pantaloons. That employee might have reminded one of stuffiness, but it goes without saying that they had set standards which many had failed to live up to.

He stopped in his musings when he realized that he may be making his son uncomfortable. So he turned to him.

(Recall 4b)
"Who started this Public Servant business in appointments? He asked his son.

"I cannot give the historical details about it," Juaning said, "but I suppose it started with the germ of an idea spread by one who now appears to be an anonymous moralist. This man wrote a public pulse column saying among others that employees in the government service should be made to appreciate the importance of their positions in the light of being called public servants. believe this man gave reasons which struck a sympathetic chord in a newspaper publisher's heart who immediately editorialized on the man's letter. Before we knew it the idea had caught national attention, not to say the attention of the President who forthwith dignified the spreading idea by proclaiming in one of his executive orders that from that time on government employees should be called public servants. The executive order was widely publicized. The government printing house published it together with several theses written about it by eminent thinkers of the nation. Since then any person who receives an appointment to the government service has been called public servant.

"It's quite amazing," he said. "But what has been done so far? What effects has it made?"

Well, for one, government employees have acquired a certain degree of pride in their positions," Juaning pointed out. "With it the efficiency that is expected of them upped. Where before they were haughty, they became modest and courteous. They no longer thought themselves as kings in their small domains. They are now servants, and they are serving the good of the people."

"Are public servants any better after the government employees were called public servants?" he asked.

"Public services are now better than ever before." Juaning said. "No backlogs in work had been reported. Correspondence are attended with dispatch, red tape is a thing of the past. Follow-ups are no longer needed because a certain service requested is met immediately. You may not believe it but even judges are up-to-date in their dockets."

"You may not believe it" Juaning continued, "but an inquiry made by a common tao (person), let's say this hour, receives a reply in the next hour. The public's satisfaction is always foremost on the mind of the public servant. This is only one example. But you should know the other wonders which this thing has wrought. The work of government is now going on smoothly like a well-oiled machine. There may be breakdowns in some cases, but these are always attended to immediately. For instance, something goes wrong in one office. Trouble shooters go to the scene at once. These trouble shooters are experts in their respective lines. If the trouble occurs, say at an education department, it is an expert on education that works on it."

"That's wonderful." he said "But how do we get to be a public servant? Does one need a recommendation from a powerful politician? Does he need pull? Does one have to be close the appointing power?"

"The method of recruitment that we have now in the civil service is an infallible system." Juaning said. "And the government didn't have to make any change in the civil service law. I has been provided in that law since it was passed many, many years back. They have just to follow the law to recruit the best through examination."

"How about these examinations?" he asked. "Before I left for abroad they had that bar scandal. There was cheating in the bar exams. A little before that there was cheating in a southern city where the examinees placed answers to questions in the examinations in sandwiches. Are these things still happening?"

"They are now things of the past, father," Juaning assured him. "I just can't tell you how it is being done because I'm not in on it, but for the past several years nothing of the sort had happened. And it wouldn't happen as can be attested by me who took a government examination recently and passed it."

"Indeed the word public servant had wrought miracles." he said.

"Yes,   it   had."   Juaning   said.

Chapter 5 -Civil Service Eligibilities

As they drove on at the speed of 40 kph, the rate of speed that the car can only go because of the built-in speed governor, father and son had an ample time to talk with each other, exchange views on sundry topics, disagreed on some points which they later threshed out but in all instances their minds met. Juanito Esguerra more often than not gave his son an affectionate look if only to confirm that their being look-alikes transcend the physical aspects.

"You must be a first grade service eligible, " he said as he groped for a topic to discuss with his son.

"Sort of," Juaning said. "But not really. People like us who have taken the professional examinations still have to avail of special law to be considered as civil service eligible. In my case, I had to avail of Republic Act 1080 to be considered as a first grader. But I didn't have to because I am holding a position that is appropriate to the civil service eligibility I possess." Juaning paused, then asked: "You are a first grader, aren't you, father?"

"Yes, I am," he said. "I am a professional engineer."

"How stupid of me," Juaning said. "I know all along that you are a professional mechanical engineer and I failed to put two and two together. I'm sorry, father."

"It's all right son," he said. "You see I passed First Grade examination before the P.M.E. examinations. By the way, are eligibilities still made to prescribe?

"I really don't know," Juaning answered. "Maybe. Why?" "I cannot seem to understand why a person who has qualified in a civil service examination be deprived of it after a certain period of time just because he failed to serve when called. It strikes me as unfair and unreasonable."

"The way to look at it," Juaning said, "I am inclined to agree with the authorities. You see, when a civil service eligible fails to serve when called, he is not only giving another civil service eligible who ranks next to him a hard time to get an appointment but also makes himself party to a conspiracy that is not of his own making."

"How would you explain that?" he asked.

"Let's take for instance a civil service eligible whom some people do not want to appoint for one reason or another," Juaning said. "When he makes inquiries if he would get an appointment or not, these people could just tell him that he is not within reach of certification, and for all he knows the persons who are working against him can validly claim so because the civil service eligible who is one rank higher than him has not yet replied to the call to serve."

"But suppose he has never been called to serve?" He asked.

"Under the civil service system," Juaning said, "I think that is impossible."

"Well, if the system is good, it is all right. But even so," he said, "there is still the possibility that he cannot be called to serve."

"The prescription period is, I believe, usually two years." he said. "Which is too short. If there should be any prescription at all, it should be made in a matter of five years. Then that would be fair to all."

"I think you're right, father," Juaning said. "Come to think of it. I guess we have just wasted our breaths discussing it. You may not know it and I may not know it, but I suppose these eligibilities, these civil service eligibilities are permanent. To put it another way, they are for life."

"Yes," he said. "I suppose so. But what made you think so?"

"A fellow government appointee told me the other day that he had obtained his civil service eligibility many, many years ago and this was the first time he had accepted an appointment in the government service."

"Really?" he said. "How come?"

"He was immediately employed after graduation by a private firm," Juaning said. "That was a year before the results of his examinations were released. He hasn't been able to avail of his eligibility because the private firm wouldn't dispense with his services when he tried to resign. They offered him better pay and opened for him a bright future. He rose from junior engineer in the firm to assistant general manager. He has recently retired from the private firm."

"You know this case of my fellow appointee," Juaning continued, "is one reason why there is a move in the government civil service to do away with permanency of civil service eligibilities. Just take this man. He had spent the best of his professional life in a private firm. Can he offer any more of it to the government? I mean, can he still give the government his best when he already relinquished much of it to the private firm?"

"You have a good point there son," he said. "But then I was not talking about permanent civil service eligibilities."

"Of course not," Juaning said. "I was just trying to slip in my ideas."

"Go on," he said.

"I also believe that making a civil service eligibility permanent is quite unfair," Juaning continued. "An examination on certain subject given today could be a whale of a difference from an examination on the same subject many years ago. Time is not the only factor that counts here but also factors like changes and developments. For instance, the examiners many years back might have fielded a question which would be anachronistic if fielded today."

"And again I have an inkling that a relative reason is also being invoked, although it is not actually permanency, in the move that some quarters are making for the repeal of Republic Act 1080 and the laws. Under these laws, people who have passed the bar and the professional examinations can apply for the conversion of their eligibilities into first grade eligibilities. In other words, they would become eligible without the benefit of taking another examination. Which had been deemed unfair. I don't know how far this move would go. I just don't know. If I know our people too well, the move might not even reach first base."

"If it's good," he said, "it should be pursued to the fullest."

Chapter 6 - Assembly Line Gov't Service

It would have been good for both father and son to stop talking to each other for a while, but both seemed to be eager to talk with each other even if it took them long to bring the chicken to roost.

"You are at present in the service of the government," he asked Juaning. "Has government service improved?"

"Very much improved," Juaning said. "You should see a government office one of these days and prove it yourself."

"Improved government service came into being with the application of the principle involved in the assembly line method," Juaning said.

"You mean the Ford idea?" he asked.

(Fig.VI-1. Let war be declared against red tape! Why not discharge customs cargo directly from the ship into the broker's truck, thence to a clearing zone where the customs team can open the crate, inspect and appraise the contents? Consignee can forthwith pay the duty declared and clear the cargo in a matter of a few hours. Courtesy of Bobby Elizes-artist.)

"Yes, the Ford idea of using assembly line methods in the production of his automobiles," Juaning said. "That man was a genius. You know, with the assembly line he was able to bring his automobiles within easy reach of the American public by making the most cars at the least cost and fastest time. He was also able to raise the wages of his employees to such a degree that they were then considered as the highest in the world. In fact until now auto workers still receive much more than most other workers in other U.S. industries. Ford's greatest legacy to mankind is the assembly line idea."

"Applied to the government service, the assembly line method has done a lot of wonders. Take any government office now existing, a government office where one obtains a license or permit, or pay his taxes or otherwise goes to that office to be served because he is a taxpayer. As soon as one enters this office, he is given a systematic check list on which are designated numbered stations where he would go to have his papers acted upon. Each of these stations is manned by two employees one of whom takes over the other's work when the other is not present in order to insure the continuity of service. A number of these stations are under the charge of a coordinator or expediter. This way a sort of conveyor system is installed that expedites the business of the paying public."

"Again let's take another office, this time let's say at the bureau of customs. Soon we may go there to get your unaccompanied cargo and soon you will be able to see how fast they are working there now. People there now work so fast that you could anything get from a ship in less than 2 hours, providing you are not taking out big shipments."

"They do it this way. Before the arrival of the boat on which you have your cargo, the bureau of customs advises you to prepare all necessary documents. The bureau also requests your broker's trucks to receive the cargo directly from the boat's cranes. As soon as the cargo is loaded on the broker's truck, it is taken to the clearing section where the crate is opened and its contents examined and appraised. Consignees are advised to be ready to pay the duties and taxes on their cargoes to cashiers detailed in the clearing section. Once the consignees had paid their duties and taxes, the gate pass is issued and the broker's trucks forthwith speed to the consignee's bodega. This procedure only takes a matter of few hours. And it satisfies everybody. The government gets its taxes while the consignees get their goods on time. There is no gainsaying he fact that the delay in release of cargoes at the bureau of customs makes a lot of consignees go into a lot of expense. Delay makes the difference between profit and loss."

"Almost all government offices had adopted the assembly line method. Let's take the Central Bank, or instance. A businessman who needs a CB license goes to the premiere banking institution for it. Before he is shuffled into the grist mill, he is first furnished all the information regarding the requirements for obtaining the license. If he possesses all these requirements, he is made to accomplish certain forms to which he is made to attach all the documents meeting the requirements. The application is received at one window and passed over to the processors who go over it with a fine-toothed comb. Once processed, the necessary license is prepared for the signature of the department head. Hardly has the ink on the department head's signature dries when one receives his license."

"Private companies had adopted the method ahead of the government. The other day I was at the insurance company where I was applying for a loan. After making some inquiries I decided to defer getting the loan because at the time I was in a great hurry. The man at the insurance company inquired how great was my hurry. I told him. He told me that I would be able to get my check in 20 minutes. Assured, I filed my loan application. You won't believe it but I really got my loan in 15 minutes."

"Have they perfected the method?" he asked.

"Yes and no," replied Juaning. "Yes in the case of offices with middling capacities of work. And no in bigger offices. There occur breakdowns but they are always prepared for them. The fact of the matter is that every big office has a special staff whose only job is to trouble-shoot. If something goes wrong along the line they are always on hand.

"The assembly line method in rendering government service has had its beneficial effects. It has cut down graft to a minimum. It is

(Fig.VI-2. **Have our bureaucrats ever heard of Henry Ford who creatively originated the assembly line method in production? Why not install a conveyor, figuratively or literally, in critical government bureaus and offices to expedite public service?   Courtesy   of   Bobby   Elizes-artist.**)

fool-proof. It is a matter of either you have it or you don't. If you need the service of the government which you feel you always do, you can get full satisfaction from any government office any time of day."

"Has the method been able to eliminate bribery?" he asked.

"Bribery is already a thing of the past. It is no longer a joke to say that one could be easily attended to in government offices by greasing some palms. Whose palms would be greased could easily be   known   in   the   final   reckoning."

Chapter 7 - Delicadeza (Righteous Self-Esteem)

Bribery a thing of the past? Juanito could not believe his ears. But then his son could not be lying, nor could he be pulling his leg. Nevertheless, he could not help but wonder and make remembrances of things past.

He remembered very well how one bribed his way into so many things in the past. He had to give a bribe of one peso to obtain a fifty centavo residence certificate just so he would not be inconvenienced by queuing to a window. He had to bribe the policeman not to issue him a ticket for committing a minor traffic violation. In fact he had to bribe almost everybody just to get service that he could otherwise obtain for free.

Bribe-giving and bribe-taking in those days flourished presumably because of inroads made by decadent elements in the morals of the people. Where before men would kill themselves just so their honor would not be tainted, men sought positions where they could be in the forefront of the messy situation. Men scrambled and schemed just to be placed in such revenue collecting agencies as the Bureau of Internal Revenue and the Bureau of Customs. Worse, men pledged their very souls.

He mulled on this festering sore of the national morals at the time and concluded that it must have begun in a very small way. People long for convenience. A slight incursion into this longing makes them devise ways, foul or fair, so they won't be made to face up to it. They start by giving gifts, small ones, gifts that would make others feel quite compensated indeed. Succeeding at it and feeling remorse for having given little, they resolve to make up for the deficiency in the next time around. On the other hand, the receiving end enjoys the way it is being lionized, and like the gift-bearer his appetite is whetted. This process carried out so many times over more often than not ends in giving and receiving better idea, and by better means turning the gifts into cash.

Several remedies have been suggested to be applied to this ailment but none seemed quite effective as nipping the whole thing in the bud. Which reminded him of a former superior in the government service. His superior had always made it a point during his incumbency to take a leave of absence from the time Christmas season sets in into way past the new year. His superior confided that he always take his leave because he wanted to avoid receiving gifts. The man knew too well what gifts mean even if given out of goodwill. This man had "delicadeza" (righteous self-esteem) which turns green whenever he was made a recipient of a gift. He had he integrity which at that time was becoming rare.

After the enlightening explanation his boss gave him, he began thinking of how to imbue "delicadeza" into the rank and file of government employees without so much as infringing into their rights. He had proposed that during Christmas season entrances to government offices should be manned by security guards whose duty it would be to stop gift-giving people from entering the government office building. This may not stop the bearer of gifts from bringing gifts to the government employee's residence, but at least it would help in minimizing the eroding effect of gift taking. This would in turn may help in imbuing in the government employees a semblance of "delicadeza". So bribery is already a thing of the past, he told himself as he glanced at his son. Maybe the people specially the government employees had finally developed a sense of "delicadeza".

Chapter 8 - Sidewalks & Pedestrian Lanes

Juanito Esguerra took time out to look at the scenery as their car cruised along the boulevard. The "tambulilid", the dwarfish coconut trees, that lined the boulevard appeared as if they were playing hopscotch from the running car. The hibiscus shrubs heavy with flowers looked as if they were all dressed up for a holiday. Everything looked pretty and happy, and everybody taking the morning walk looked free and gay, enjoying the kind sun tapping its rays on their heads. But what made him sat up and noticed are the sidewalks where people could hike freely, body erect, head high, swinging their arms along.

At any time of day many years ago any street in the country's cities and centers of population, one found people walking the streets, exposing themselves to the danger of losing their life or limb by getting bumped or ran over by the onrushing motor vehicles. The reason for this was that most, if not all, the country's metropolitan areas lacked enough sidewalks. Or if there were any, the sidewalks were either too narrow to carry a normal load of pedestrians that people perforce just spilled into the streets and used the highways as walks.

(Fig. VIII-1. How can there be recognition and dignification of the human personality if there are no sidewalks where man can walk freely, arms swinging, body erect, looking forward, head high, creative thoughts flowing upwards? Courtesy of Bobby Elizes, artist.)

The sidewalk situation in the country then was indeed deplorable that any native who had gone to foreign lands could not help but let off steam on it and remarking loudly that native city planners had still a lot to learn from their counterparts in other countries.

By design, most city planners in other countries made it a point to have wide enough sidewalks in their cities to accommodate the heavy pedestrian traffic even during the so-called rush hours without people using the streets as walks. The discerning visitor, using the sidewalk in his tour, could easily form the opinion that the concrete pavement on which he was treading was not just an adjunct to the street but an essential part of it.

Moreover, the visitor begins to form other ideas in his mind as his awe for the wide sidewalks grows. When the dimensions of this sidewalk were taken into consideration by the city planner, he starts telling himself, he equated them to a constant: people. Men, women, and children. People who are going to use it in traveling from one place of the city to the other. People whose safety he put over and above all.

Did our city planners have the people's safety in their minds when they designed the sidewalks? He asked himself then. And he got his answer from a cursory study of the city sidewalks.

At the time he had allowed his opinion to be disputed by one who must know his history as well as his rhetoric. He allowed his disputant to say that the city planners then had little or no hand at all in the making of most of the sidewalks. They were the carry-overs of ancient plans which have not spared even the streets.

Granting without admitting that this was true, he had argued, why then was not anything done when revisions of these ancient plans were made? Did the city planners had the people in mind? Maybe, but they were not the kind of people who were given consideration because they were the property owners slivers on whose lots would be taken to form part of the sidewalk. But then property owners were people too!

Then there was the tolerance the city authorities gave the occupancy of the sidewalks by rude and uncouth ambulant vendors. This had aggravated the situation of the sidewalks. At the time one could never find a city sidewalk without a vendor hogging part of it.

But then he had hoped that in spite of the seemingly hopeless state of Philippine sidewalks, taxpayers could still hope for better times, and he didn't have to join a Movement for Better and Wider Sidewalks to make the hope spring eternal. All the citizen could do then, he opined, was to flood the authorities with suggestions that more or less hewed to the following lines:

1   Request city planners to design wider and better sidewalks.

2   Request city planners to place the people's safety over and above when they are made to choose between an aggrieved property owner and a wider sidewalk.

3   Request the law-abiding councils or cities and population centers to pass ordinances aimed at prodding city planners to design wider and better sidewalks.

4   Request police departments to enforce the law or ordinance, if there is any, penalizing persons who unscrupulously appropriate parts of sidewalks for places of business no matter how legitimate.

5   Address appeals to civic organization to work out plans that would make our sidewalks a better place to walk on.

6   Henceforth the Bureau of Public Highways shall be known as the Bureau of Public Highways and Sidewalks.

7   Man is more important than any of his creations. The automobile being only one of man's creations can never be more important than man himself. The sidewalk is more important than the street or highway.

These suggestions, interminably drummed into the heads of the authorities concerned, might wake up the city's elders and open their eyes to the worsening sidewalk situation.

These he did think of many years ago. Now all of them seemed to have been followed.

He was in the heart of the city, feeling the pulse of the metropolis. It was wonderful to be back in the old country, a nation whose face had changed much during the years. He was quite overwhelmed by the changes that he had seen with his own eyes: the wide sidewalks, the one-way streets, the no-parking areas. These were the exceptions many years ago. Then there was no regard for the individual. Everything seemed geared to the machine, that infernal machine known as the automobile. But now it is different.

He was awed by the pedestrian lanes he found at almost every street corner, and as this fact gradually made him aware of the improvements that had been made on the face of the city, he began asking questions of himself.

Who is now the city mayor?

What ordinances had he caused to be passed by the city council?

What civic improvements had he done?

What contributions had he made to the ultimate glory of the individual?

These ruminations had again clearly etched in his questioning mind the fact of the pedestrian lane.

Pedestrian lanes we must have, he said. They give dignity to the man on the street, raise him over and above he iron-clad motor vehicles.

Who started all this anyway but man, he said to himself. If it is man who had been responsible for the creation of these machines, then it must be man who should be placed on a pedestal, not the iron machine.

Many years ago, the automobiles ruled the streets. Everything seemed geared to his perpetuation of this part of the planet. Traffic rules and regulations were more often drawn up and hewed close to the transit of these machines. No stone was left unturned to make this man's creation get a better lot than the individual, than man himself.

He had argued for the pedestrian lanes because he believed that they were part and parcel of man's life. It is the dividing line, the line that separates the man, who must be master over all, and the automobile. Besides it was one way of asserting man's superiority over the machine.

The pedestrian lane was also the source of pride of the man on the street. To it the pedestrian could point out with pride that somehow a space is reserved for him in the automobile-dominated streets.

Aside from these arguments, however, there were still other considerations to be taken in hand. Who, for instance, must be given priority in our streets? The pedestrian or the car-riding man?

Seeing those pedestrian lanes on almost every street really made him swell with pride. Man has finally been given his proper place. His importance in the scheme of things has finally been given due credit. He recalled Dr. Jose P. Laurel who said that the great tragedy today is that the common man is not given the recognition and dignification due him.

Chapter 9 - Government Bids

Juanito whistled as the car joined another stream of motor vehicles. He always whistled when he felt glad, when he felt there was something to be happy about. Hearing his father whistle, Juaning turned to him and smiled.

"Happy, father?" he asked.

"Yes," he said. "I am happy to be back in this country which had changed for the better a lot since I left."

"I am happy for you, too, father," Juaning said.

"Thank you, son," he said.

They had come into the main stream of the traffic when he made a request of his son.

"Can you drive around before heading for home?"

"Gladly, father," Juaning said. "I'll show you the city, the new city, the better city that you left many years ago."

Juaning steered clear of the traffic and went into a side street. Then he made a turn and headed for the Port Area. Juanito Esguerra was still trying to figure out where his son was taking the car when he made a wild guess.

"You're heading for the piers?" he asked.

"Yes," said Juaning. "That's where we will start." The piers were quite memorable to him. They reminded him of the job he used to do for the government. It also relived the days when he worked in that place for a big foreign company selling equipment.

"Hey," he suddenly said.

"Hey, what, father?" Juaning asked.

"As an electrical engineer, have you ever tried drafting the specifications of equipment which you may need in your work?" he asked.

"No," Juaning replied. "I worked for a different department. But why do you ask, father?"

"I just wanted to know how they go about preparing specifications," He said. "Are they still up to their necks playing tricks on their suppliers?"

"I don't know what you mean by tricks, father," Juaning said, "but I believe the people who handle the preparation of specifications in our department and in other departments, for that matter, do it on the level."

"You know, son," he said, "in the past, many government employees in charge of preparation of specifications for equipment and supplies to be purchased by the government draft them in a clever manner that only an equipment, a particular equipment handled by a certain company, is favored. Specifications were so worded that more often than not they become no less than purchase orders for known products. They were done so that only one bidder would win. This gives rise to the suspicion that somehow an under the table deal had been agreed upon. There must be kickbacks in the deal, horse-trading involving the you-scratch-my-back-and-I'll-scratch-yours agreements, or anything that is irregular and anomalous."

"At the time, there was an instance when the man in charge of making the specifications in a certain government office demanded that a diesel electric set his office was going to buy should have an engine with a certain bore and a certain stroke! Those who read the specifications knew at once that a deal between a known supplier and the man in charge of purchases in that particular office was a-cooking. One didn't have to stretch his imagination to know so. But one question screwed the curiosity of the prospective losing bidders: Is the electricity produced by an engine with a specified bore and stroke different from that produced by an engine of another bore and stroke? Is there another kind of electricity?'

"Did those things really happen then?" Juaning asked.

"Of course, they did happen, son," he said.

And because they did happen, he had then proposed that all specifications prepared by government agencies carry the following clause:

"Nothing in the above specifications shall be construed to mean that a particular brand or make is favored. Any equipment or supplies of whatever brand or make substantially complying with the specifications which have been successfully demonstrated to perform the work or serve he purpose for which it is intended in accordance with good engineering practice, to the satisfaction of the government, will be considered."

He was not sure yet whether his clause or anything like it has been integrated in all government specifications, but he was inclined to believe that something had been done to correct the past shenanigans. If it is true that all government specifications are now being prepared on the level, as Juaning had just said a little while ago, then there really had been a great change in the scheme of things.

He recalled another well known trick: to require immediate delivery. Before the war, the great President Manuel L. Quezon, in his inimitable way of preventing graft, required that all equipment and long range supplies to be requisitioned by the government shall be for delivery in not more than 120 days, except in cases where loss of life and/or property is involved. This wise regulation made the government officials far-sighted insofar as their requirement for equipment and supplies is concerned, and the best price could be obtained from the suppliers. Seldom was a cooked-up deal possible.

Chapter 10 - Trip Cutting

Juaning drove the car at a reasonable slow speed so that his father could take in the scenery as they cruised towards the piers. On the way he pointed out the ubiquitous jeepney to his father.

"You must remember the jeepney, father," Juaning said. "But of course."

"Sure, sure, son," he said. "I remember the jeepney very well. Who would forget the jeepney when I took it every morning in going to work and returning home. Could I forget it? Never. I could never forget the practice of jeepney operators who bathed the non-skid floors of their jeepneys with oil in the morning. Of course, they did so to protect their property, but they forget to consider the people who would ride in the jeepneys and slide in the process."

"They no longer do it now, father," Juaning said. "They finally realized that they started losing passengers when they insisted on doing so. And these jeepney operators had improved their conveyances. These jeepneys, also buses, now have partitions on the seats. Passengers no longer crowd each other. They now have really one seat allowed each of them."

"Just why are you telling me this?" he curiously asked. "I was just reminded of an article you wrote on jeepney drivers, particularly their nefarious practice of trip cutting. No one made them to stop it. They just suddenly did not resort to it anymore. I just don't know why. Presumably because of a subject they took up starting from fourth grade of the elementary school. They call it H.H.R. or something like it."

Just what was Juaning referring to when he mentioned about the article and jeepneys and trip cutting. He tried to remember what it was. Finally it dawned on him that he had actually written an article about trip cutting, and it more or less ran this way:

"This is a daily event:

"A man rushes to his place of work to beat the cold and steely Bundy clock that efficiently ticks out the time. At the street corner where he takes his jeep he finds a lot of people who, for all he knows, also have the same thing that is on his mind: beat a Bundy clock, a feat which, before they accomplish it, would require them to beat each other to the first jeepney that comes along."

"The first jeepney comes along and our man is able to take it. He feels heartened. Now he can beat that efficient Bundy clock. But no sooner had he spoken when the jeepney driver announces that he could only take his passengers as far. Our man makes a protest which is readily squelched by the jeepney driver who firmly, arrogantly says that our man could take another jeepney which he knows may come a long time yet. Our man agrees. At the end of his trip our man takes another jeepney whose driver pulls the same trick. Al told he takes three or four rides which could ordinarily be made in one just going to the office to beat he Bundy clock."

"This is a daily event, and it happens to our man multiplied one thousand, nay, ten-thousand times."

"At first blush, a self righteous man would think worse of the opportunistic driver. He may even consider laying a hand on the unscrupulous fellow, or bashing the vulture's head with the lunch box. Indeed he may have something short of murder on his head. Indeed he may have something short of murder on his mind."

"But these thoughts suddenly vanish as another thought showing that carrying out any of them could only result in a pyrrhic victory forms in his mind. He simmers down, and contemplating the beautiful sari-manok (rooster) patterns on the jeepney's sky-roof, he preoccupies himself with thoughts of fighting off the incursions of the jeepney driver into his measly daily allowance with means that some people may be slow to catch on but which may prove to be very effective in the long run."

"One recourse that would be open to him in declaring hostilities on the trip cutting jeepney driver is the boycott. He could stop riding the jeepney of the trip cutter and convince several others to do the same. Jeepney drivers are out to earn their daily bread and a move that would mean the loss of fares for him would naturally make him think twice before engaging in trip cutting. The boycott was effective in the United States when its first settlers yelled for taxation with representation. It proved to be the best weapon for the Chinese when the neighboring country of Japan was flooding China cities with cheap merchandise. Our man can take a lesson from these historical facts."

"Our man could also report the matter to the first police officer he finds, and the police officer would take care of the rest. If there is no officer in sight, he could make a citizen arrest. Under the law a plain citizen could make an arrest if he knows that a felony has been committed."

"Or our man could inform the public service commission in writing about the trip cutting activity, citing the owner of the public conveyance. Doubtlessly the public service commission would act on his information and/or complaint immediately."

"In any case, our man should take the matter up by its horns and grapple with it. Allowing unscrupulous practice to flourish would only lead jeepney drivers to more serious offenses and dire forebodings."

"Trip cutting as brazenly practiced by a majority of jeeney drivers is sad commentary on the moral tone set by the fast changing times. It seems that man, caught in the cross-currents caused by an insuperable materialistic tide, has to devise ways and means of survival. Putting one over the other or taking advantage of the weakness of another points out an easy way out of the predicament; and trip cutting for the jeepney driver is one means he could use quite effectively."

"Short of recommending a complete overhaul of our moral values, one can think of nothing that would at least minimize, if not eliminate, trip cutting. But then the situation is not entirely hopeless. Somehow a solution may be arrived at. In the meantime, we can fight this evil with the limited resources we have at hand."

The situation then was not entirely hopeless, he thought. The fact that jeepney drivers no longer resort to trip cutting more than proves the point.

Chapter 11 - Playground In The Streets

It was wonderful seeing the city and getting the feel of it again. It was an experience, a great experience for him. As they drove through the streets he noticed that familiar scenes and sights and sounds were no longer around. The sidewalk vendors who used to hug the sidewalks were nowhere to be found. Ugly newsstands no longer obstructed the sidewalks. No urchins assaulted them to sell assorted wares from cigarettes to newspapers. From where he sat in the car he could see a clear view of the busy street corner several blocks away.

He also noticed that the children no longer played in the streets as was their wont in the residential areas that they passed. No children tug or play "tumbang preso", He saw no child play hopscotch or a boy fly a kite. Even the once familiar basketball court set up in the streets by obliging politicians were no longer around.

He wanted to tell himself that he did not see what he was expecting to see presumably because the children were either busy doing something else or they may be engaged in childish occupation that confined them to their houses. But then school was out, a sign that there should now be a swarm of children all over the streets. Moreover, children won't be engaging in their childish preoccupations all at the same time.

The scenes simply didn't ring a bell. In other words, they seem extraordinary and unusual, and he groped for an explanation.

"Miss anything, father?" Juaning asked. A smile hung on the boy's lips as if he were keeping something away from his father.

"Yes," He answered. "I'm missing something. Many years ago these streets rang with children's laughter, children playing in the streets. Are they producing no children anymore?"

"Of course not," Juaning said. "There are still thousands of children in this neighborhood."

"But I haven't seen anyone yet," he said.

"Yes, there are no children around," the son said. "Not right now anyway. If I am not mistaken they are now in the playgrounds."

"A playground in this neighborhood?" he was amazed. "Yes," Juaning said. "Every neighborhood now has a playground. We will see one as soon as we turn the corner."

The playground was wide and spacious. Every known plaything that children can play with was in the playground. Slides, seesaws, swings and what have you that delight the children. And the children were swarming all over them.

Many years ago, he remembered, the children played in the streets. There was then a dearth of playgrounds, and if there were any, they were either far and small compared to the playground he was now seeing. It was for this reason that they played in the streets.

Once upon a time he had expressed his views on playing in the streets. It was unjust, unfair, and constituted foul play in the first water. He was not blaming the children for it. Rather he was condemning the children's elders and their parents as well as the government.

Parents should never tolerate their children to play in the streets. It is not so much the danger and the nuisance but what the habit will do to the character of the child. A child used to playing in the streets without compunction will grow up into an adult who has no healthy respect for public property, one who thinks the street is an extension of his living room, a nuisance to pedestrians and motorists, a potential squatter, who will build his shanty in any available vacant lot, whether private or public, without the benefit of permission from anybody. Too much untrammeled playing in the streets as a child have exacted its toll --his recognition of private and public ownership of real estate is hazy.

It is unjustifiable to allow children to play in the streets, he had said. For one, the children were risking life and limb playing in the streets. They were likewise posing a potent cause for traffic accidents, not to mention other kinds of accidents.

He had transmitted his views to his friends, people he knew could apply remedies, civic spirited citizens, community leaders, even the powers that be in government. His friends commiserated with him while others agreed with his views. But that was as far as they went. They said they would do something about the problem and stopped there. They really did nothing to his disgust.

But now he had seen a change, indeed a great change to the whole picture. And he was glad. He looked at his son wanting to know what happened when he was away. What events transpired during his absence to bring about this almost utopian scene. But his son   had   his   mind   elsewhere.

Chapter 12 - Vacant Lots

Juaning drove around the city, passing through the business district, through the maze of commercial establishments to the residential districts. Except for areas that were reserved for playgrounds, parks and plazas, each lot that they passed was either occupied by a tall building or a residential home.

This was not the case many years ago, he thought, when it was the fashion to make lots remain vacant. The idea then was to speculate. It was really an era of speculators, both petty and big time, people who preyed on other people's needs and circumstances. He remembered well the case of a big industrialist and land developer who bought land in the suburbs east of the city. The man was able to get reasonable prices for the first set of lots he purchased, but as he looked around for more land to make his project complete, he found that land prices had risen. Because he wanted the land to make his dream of developing the area materialize, he had to buy at the prices dictated by the sellers. However, he came to a saturation point, a point where he had to check himself, a point where he decided not to buy anymore than at the price he believed was reasonable to him. This decision left several lot owners holding the bag. Because these lot owners could no longer sell their lots at a lower price and the buyer could not go any higher, the lots became isolated.

Thinking of that case he could not help but be amused because he saw with his own eyes the situation of the lots. They looked like islands in a sea of developed lots, a monument, it seemed to the stupidity of some people.

But that was not what made him apprehensive of land speculators.

What are land speculators anyway but humans who are out to make a profit, for wasn't it just human to profit out of something? The enormity of the profit is immaterial. What he was afraid of is the effect it has on the general well-being of the people.

Speculation led to undeveloped lots and undeveloped lots contributed to retrogression. A series of undeveloped lots along the highway, taken together, add up to retrogression. They make costs rise. The cost of communication and transportation, the cost of essential services --all of these things rise.

He was engaged in these ruminations when Juaning broke the silence between them.

"A penny for your thoughts." Juaning said.

"I was thinking," he said. "So many things have changed in the country since I left. So many changes had been wrought. These houses and buildings, for instance. These occupied lots."

"It is really surprising to see how these houses and buildings sprouted," he said. "If I am not mistaken they are the result of the campaign conducted in the country telling how much people could help in the national effort to bring economic prosperity by developing vacant lots and lands and improving already developed estates. The campaign met with indifference at the outset, but as it gathered momentum as well as popularity, land development became a necessity because of the enactment of a law raising the real estate tax on unimproved residential land to the level of improved land."

"What happened?" he asked.

"Speculators found it worthwhile to sit on unimproved residential lots to await higher prices. They had to sell to the developers in quick time. The developers had a better break which ultimately benefited the home buyer."

"Years ago," Juanito reminisced, "it was simply impossible for the average working man to own a house and lot under the conditions then obtaining."

"A great President who unfortunately died in the middle of his term brought about the turning point," Juanito explained. "This great President said that those who have less in life should have more in law. The little man is fundamentally entitled a little more food in his stomach, a little more clothing on his back and a little more roof over his head. What a credo!"

"What   a   President"   Juanito   exclaimed.

Chapter 13 - Schoolhouses

As they rounded up a corner to turn into another street, he noticed the public school building a few houses away. Built along modern lines, it was very much an improvement of the schoolhouses in the past.

"Is it true that there are enough schoolhouses now that are needed by schoolchildren?" he asked his son.

"Yes, there is no more schoolhouse problem," Juaning replied. "Do you remember the time that school children had to be packed into ugly Quonset huts or make-shift buildings made out of nipa shingles? The picture has changed now. You should see the school houses in the barrios. They are a far cry from what they were in the past."

"Really?" he said. "So there are now enough schoolhouses to accommodate all the school children."

Before he left for a foreign country, the state of school houses in the nation was sad. What was sadder was the fact that sometimes there were no school houses to be sad about. There was indeed a dearth of school buildings. But it seems the problem was solved both ends. The building of school houses was accelerated and the number of school children was decelerated by planned parenthood.

It was the practice then of the department of education authorities to lease private buildings to house the school children. At most these buildings could offer no more than the space where the desks and tables are placed. The other facilities needed in a school had to be neglected.

For a building to be a good school house, it has to have the minimum facilities of a school. Space, play areas, comfort rooms, romper rooms ---in fact rooms for every conceivable activity that the school children engage in while in school. But the schools then, that is, the schools located in private buildings didn't have these facilities.

Furthermore, the money being spent in renting these private buildings or schools was like money going down the drain. It was a matter of common knowledge that the government could build several school houses with the money it was spending on the rent. Why then this method of housing school children? One could only speculate why. There had been mysterious goings on in the leases of private buildings for private offices. The mystery might have seeped into the school system.

"How did this come about?" he asked Juaning.

"What?"

"More school buildings for less increase of school children

due to family planning."

He remembers too well the statement of the chairman of the House Appropriations Committee: "The supply of school houses cannot keep pace with the increase in the number of school children."

"I really don't know how it all started." his son replied. "But once there was an agitation made by the parents and the teachers for the building of school houses. They wrote their congressmen. They swamped the office of the President with letters to the effect that more school houses should be built. At first their pleas fell on deaf ears. But then they started putting in subtle threats into their letters like voting for their opponents in the coming election, then the congressmen were galvanized into action. No self-respecting congressman at the time stood in the halls of Congress without saying anything about the school house problem. Before we knew it, the school houses were proliferating in the countryside."

"And that's how it came about," his son said.

He smiled. He knew for a fact that he suffered as much as the next parent when there was a dearth of school houses. Now that there are school houses, the school children could have all the opportunity   to   getting   the   best   schooling.

Chapter 14 - Teachers

The subject of schoolhouses naturally brought up the subject of the teachers. He inquired about the teachers.

"They are fine," Juaning said. "The last time I heard about the teachers, the government was fixing their salaries at the minimum of P400 a month. I know it is still low compared to the salaries highly developed countries are paying their teachers, but I think it is quite as good a start for anything that should be raised."

"Raising their salaries would help much in getting more efficiency from them," he said. "Not that I think teachers are inefficient, because I believe it is not the teacher's fault. The kind of training that they received, coupled with the pledges that they had made before they even thought of practicing the profession are I think enough to drive them to inspired heights. What I don't consider enough to sustain this drive is the salary that they are receiving."

"You know, father," Juaning said, "I believe students are only as good as their teachers. A poorly prepared teacher makes for a poorly trained student."

"Yes," he said, "I agree with you on that point. I had always believed that teachers should be well-prepared, not to say well-equipped for their chosen profession."

"Not anyone can be a good teacher. Although it is true that teachers are made, not born, it is equally true that one must be intellectually prepared before he or she is made to pursue a profession, particularly teaching. In order to be a successful teacher, one must have that essential potential, the "X", that unknown which spells the difference between a good teacher and so-so-tutor."

"All reforms must begin with the mind if we are to escape an eternity of darkness" said Rodolfo G. Tupas, one of the most notable writers of the younger generation. Nobody can do a better job of reforming the minds of our young than the teachers. Nobody can do a better job of changing the fossilized thinking and attitude of our people but teachers with adventurous and creative minds.

"And I believe this job of separating the grain from the chaff and making certain that it is the grain that gets the cup rather than the chaff should start at the teacher's school. A rigid screening should be made of people who are aspiring to be teachers. Although the procedure is being done in our best schools, yet a majority of would-be tutors who are not only ill-equipped but also quite ready to be ill-prepared are admitted into other schools because they could pay their tuition. Something should be done at the roots. Otherwise we would have something in our hands that cannot correct in several generations."

"The need for upgrading teachers and the teaching profession is imperative," he said.

"I am sure that something along that line has been done by our government," Juaning said. "As a matter of fact, the increase of salaries for teachers is only one of them. The policy now in most teacher colleges hews closely to the policy of selecting the best material for teachers. For instance, it is strictly required that one who would aspire to be a teacher has to belong to the upper thirty percent of the graduating class in the school from which he or she graduated. Not only that. The teacher aspirant must also prove that he deserves admission by the entrance examination he is made to take. And the whole thing does not end there. The teacher aspirant must maintain a certain level of academic rating, otherwise he or she gets kicked out of the school."

"The school authorities have also done away with ETC's (Elementary Teacher's Certificate) or studies leading to that academic ranking. They now have a four year course in elementary education. To be a teacher nowadays one must at least have a BS degree. Or to be exact, Bachelor of Science in Elementary Education degree (BSEEd)."

"Is that enough insurance to give more good teachers? He asked.

"In my opinion," Juaning said, "it is as much insurance as

anything else."

"I hope I could bring good tidings for the morrow." he said.

"I hope so," Juaning said. "Because by all means a good teacher is what we should have. Just to be facetious about it, allow me to quote the writer who said, 'When a doctor makes a mistake, he buries it; when an architect makes a mistake, he covers it with ivy; but when a teacher makes a mistake, he may become a member of the school board.'"

Let us stop perpetuating the mistake and perhaps we will at least stop sliding down. Let us up-grade the quality of our teachers and perhaps the whole nation will begin to go up. "A chain is no stronger   than   its   weakest   link."

Chapter 15 - Sanctity of Domicile

"Shall we head for home now, son?" he asked Juaning.

"At your pleasure, father," Juaning said. "We are only a few minutes' drive from home."

Home was a medium-size house in a Manila suburb. A two-story house of mixed materials, it looked solid and quite livable.

"This is the house, father," Juaning said as he stopped the car.

The first thing that he noticed about the house is that it was quite different from that which he left more than fifteen years ago. It did not have the window grills which were part and parcel of houses in those days. In fact he saw nothing that reminded him of those days that one not only feared for his safety but also feared for the invasion of his home.

He believed and had always believed that next to liberty and the pursuit of happiness the sanctity of domicile is probably the most sacred in a democracy. A man's home is his castle however humble it is. It is his sanctum sanctorum, a place that guarantees for him and his family privacy, freedom from molestation, freedom from search.

He formed this belief under the influence of his father. A maestro, a teacher of old, schooled in the fast and strict rules of discipline as well as in the edifying concepts of freedom and liberty, his father used to admonish him with the quotation: "A man's home however humble is his castle. The rains may enter, the winds may enter, but the King shall not enter." His father was impressing on him the fact that no matter how humble a man's home, no one, not even the King or the highest magistrate in the land, had the right to violate its sanctity.

His father had also taught him that doors are only intended for dogs and cats and animals that are not capable of reason. Doors are open to these animals, but to the moral man, doors, whether they are open or not, are closed to him, and he could only enter them if he has the permission. Hence, one may find the main door of a house left open in the middle of the night but because such a door is figuratively closed, one must first have to knock before one could gain permission to enter.

As he grew older, he began to appreciate the advice of his father. A reading of the Constitution, the basic law of the land, and the Civil Code, had gained him the additional knowledge that his father was right and there was wisdom in his advice.

Before he left the country he had advocated the return to sanity by proposing that H.H.R. be taught in the schools in such a manner that the full meaning of the sanctity of domicile be made to sink into the minds of everyone. The screaming message which the quotation, "a man's home is his castle" must be fully impressed into the minds and hearts of every school child to make it part and parcel of his being. Once accomplished, everybody would feel safe in the confines of his home, secure within the four walls of his domicile. His house may just be a dilapidated hut, a hovel with a leaky roof, but at least he could rest assured that not even a king with all his power and his armies may gain entrance to it. And may God in His infinite wisdom always make every fiber of our being shake with dread and horror every time our hands attempt to open a door to a man's domicile without his permission!

If all the school children all over the world would memorize to their hearts the above quotation, with the full import of the meaning reaching the innermost recesses of their beings, then in about ten to fifteen years time when these children will have become the leaders of their respective peoples, aggression among nations will never again rear its ugly head!

He's back home. As he surveyed his domain with eyes and ears keen in knowing what's in it for him, he felt a sense of triumph one gets to feel when he sees that what he had been hoping for in the past had finally been realized. However, he has yet to know about the changes that had occurred while he was away.

Chapter 16 - Finish Your Plate

At the door a beautiful graying woman welcomed Juanito

Esguerra. She must be over forty but her looks belied her age. The woman was his wife Esperanza. He embraced her fondly and gave her a peck on her cheek.

"It's been a long time, mother," he said.

"Yes, quite a long time," she said. Tears of joy were streaming down her cheeks.

"How's everything?" he asked in choked voice.

"Fine," she replied. "Just fine. Everything has changed for the better."

"So I noticed," he said. "Our home is different now, for one."

"Very different," she said. "But you must be tired after your trip, father."

"Not very," he said. "Just a little fagged out. I had asked Juaning to make the rounds of the city before coming here."

"But you must be famished by now," she said. "You know what? I have prepared breakfast that is typically Filipino. Sinigang (boiled vegetables), pritong tapa (fried beef), chocolate and kesong puti (carabao cheese)."

"Gosh," he said. "Show me the table."

For the first time in fifteen years he sat at table with his family and ate with them. It was his first full Filipino meal in a long time, and he tingled with thrill. In the foreign country where he had stayed for many years, he considered himself very lucky indeed if he could have a modicum of what would pass for a Filipino meal. A haphazardly done adobo (pork dish), an uncertain pinakbet (vegetable dish), a tasteless sinigang (boiled vegetable) and other Filipino dishes prepared in such a manner as to make the average Filipino housewife turn purple in rage were all what he had tasted in the foreign country. Now that he got the real McCoy, he hungered for more. He could finish the plate of sinigang and tapa, relish the kesong puti and still ask for more.

But it was sooner said than done. He found that he could not be equal to what was set against him. He wasn't able to execute his gourmandise thoughts. In fact, after feeling that he was already full, he found to his surprise his plate still messy with leftovers. This did not happen to him before. He looked at his wife's plate. It was clean. His son's plate was also clean. They did not leave anything on their plates. A question passed over his mind the answer to which was furnished by his son.

"You see, father," Juaning said, "we had learned to finish our plates even if it makes us burst. It is part of our regimen, a sort of self discipline in us, and made part and parcel of our being by HHR.

"The subject of HHR kept pounding into our heads that wasting food is criminal, just as wasting water is criminal. Food should not be taken for granted. The ingredients are costly, and their preparation and cooking take precious time and additional costs to buy the seasonings. Year in and year out our teachers tell us to finish our plates. In school parties, every school boy and girl learned by heart finishing his/her plate. It's now second nature."

"How's that again?" he asked.

Suddenly he felt ashamed. He should have exercised care in getting his food as was his habits, homecoming or not. One's eyes should never be bigger than his stomach, as the saying goes. He should have taken only what he could finish. But then it was not too late yet. He took spoon and fork again and resumed digging into his plate. He raise his eyes from what he was eating and saw smiles on the faces of his wife and son. He was pleased.

"You know what," he said, "I think both of you are right. Anyone who should take a plateful of food is expected to finish it. If he does not finish it he should be punished."

"I can just imagine a man who had suffered privations," he continued. "During his misery he must have thought up a program he would follow if he should again be fortunate to be lifted out of his suffering, and the program followed a definitive scheme grounded on the word 'enough'. He should only take what's enough for him. Enough is enough and what go beyond is either sheer stupidity or plain hoggishness."

"It is a beautiful habit taking only what's enough and what's good for oneself. It puts the foot on excesses and blunts the deleterious effects that excesses bring. Too much of anything, be it food or wine or whatever it is that you want to have much of, is bad for the constitution. It opens wide avenues for diseases to set it. It makes one prey to the ills that afflict the world, fair game to the quirks of fate."

He looked at his plate again. He had finished the food he had scooped into his plate. And he was glad. And so was his wife and   son.

Chapter 17 - Loud Radio and TV Sets

"That was a wonderful meal, mother," he said. "We should have more of it."

"You and your flattery," his wife said. "You have never changed. You always compliment me with anything I do, even if what I did is nothing short of being worse."

"You really cooked a good meal, mother," he said. "Really good. As the Americans say, it calls for another meal."

"Don't worry," she said. "I'll cook you another one, another wonderful one, to put it in your own words."

"It's a deal," he said.

His wife went to attend to her housewifely chores while he and Juaning repaired to the living room or sala to smoke. Juaning flicked the knob of the radio set on one end of the room before he took the seat near his father. As soon as the sound of music filtered out of the radio set, he suddenly remembered something.

"Son," he said, "I had observed that no radio or TV set in the neighborhood is blaring out loud. I noticed that people don't play their sets loudly anymore. Why?"

He was always curious. Since he had noted the changes on his arrival he had always been curious. He wanted to know why, nay, the whys and wherefores of the changes. He was indeed that curious. Why, for instance, is this thing which was being done this way many years not being done that way anymore. What made the change? How did the change come about? Questions, probing questions that cried for answers, swirled in his head, swirled like myriads of stars asking to be discovered.

Juaning's answer to his question was quite simple, too simple indeed to be believed, too devoid of the pompous to be true.

"They just don't want to disturb their neighbors," Juaning replied. "Well, yes. That is all there is to it. They don't like to disturb their neighbors."

"They won't want to disturb the neighbors?" he asked himself. "It is amazing. Many years ago people don't care if their neighbors died of the noise they were creating."

He was not satisfied with Juaning's answer. He wanted to needle him more, but Juaning was ready for it.

"But of course," Juaning said. "It took sometime before people were able to cultivate the habit of not wanting to disturb their neighbors."

"It started rather gradually, imperceptibly," Juaning pursued his study. "In a certain neighborhood the people, coaxed by their children who learned from their HHR, agreed to tone down the sound of their radio and TV sets. They have learned through experience that their propensity to make their radio and TV sets blare loudly had created so much trouble for all of them. The situation has also caused so many untoward incidents."

"Quarrels among neighbors were not rare because of the loud playing of these sets. There was one time that a bitter family feud set off quarrels that set off by quarrels that rose out of these sets. But then, that was not all. People got sick because of the sometimes stupid way some of their neighbors play their radio and TV sets. They developed insomnia or some other sickness due to listening to those blaring sets."

"And again there was the time when one of the houses in

the neighborhood was visited by a second story man who carried away all the precious belongings of a family. A member of this victimized family had shouted at the top of his voice for help but none of his neighbors heard him. This case opened the eyes of the inhabitants in this neighborhood. They traced the cause to the sound blaring of the radio and TV sets.

"Faced with a problem, the neighborhood banded together. In a meeting conducted by the people in the neighborhood it was agreed that no radio and TV sets would be played loudly again."

"Nor did they stop at that. One of them, a public relations man, asked a friend to write about it. The situation received wide publicity when a widely circulated newspaper picked up the story. Upon reading of the benefits derived by the neighborhood from the discipline which they had imposed upon themselves, people from other neighborhoods decided to follow the step taken by that particular neighborhood. A chain reaction was created. Everybody began emulating the example set by that ideal neighborhood. Before one knows it, it has become a universal practice in this country."

"It ought to be," he said. "All of us suffer a certain deafness because of the world we live in. The noise that assails our ears once we take a step out of our homes is dinning. We should be easy on ourselves. We should not compound our suffering by playing these radio and TV sets aloud."

Then he began to ruminate. It was always his way. "Somewhere," he said, "somewhere I read that we city folks are hard of hearing compared to the country folks. Results of experiments conducted by eminent scientists prove it. Shall we allow ourselves to grow deafer by the loud playing of the radio and TV sets?"

"I should say not," replied Juaning. "The low sound that you hear from the radio attest to that."

"I can hear that," he said.

"I can hear that well," he said to himself. As if entranced by the soft sounds that he was hearing, he was again transported to the Utopia that he was dreaming of. Could this be the ideal country that I wanted my country to be?

Perhaps, but he still has more to know and see before he can pass judgment. One swallow do not make a summer. That was how skeptical he was. At least that was the form of skepticism that he now has born out of the frustrations he had experienced in the past.

Chapter 18 - Commercials & TV Ads With Integrity

"**That was a** fine session, son," he said after listening to the music played on a low key on the radio. "A fine session, indeed."

"Very fine, indeed," he said "Haven't you noticed anything?"

"But of course," he said. "I noticed that that there were no long commercials."

"And the commercials did not take up much of the time of the program," Juaning said.

He remembered too well the time many years ago when he made a count of the commercials that were made on a program. It was a foolhardy thing to do but because he wanted to prove something, he made a go of the project. He found that for every three minutes of listening time, the listener is also made to make himself prey to the commercials.

He discovered then that if the commercials were fresh and informative they weren't a bit irritating. But most of the commercials were just hackneyed and lousy that one could die in his seat just listening to them.

He had hankered for commercials with integrity, ones that would edify rather than make the listener feel crass. How he had rejoiced at the time on having been able to listen to a program whose creative commercial gave him a boost. It was a commercial about a new product. Nothing much was said about the product, nothing more than a few lines which served to introduce it to the buying public. The sponsor, the president of the sponsoring company himself, made the introduction. He made it so brief and so concisely that one listening to it made him look for the product.

This was in direct contrast to a TV commercial he used to see while viewing some of his favorite programs. The commercial was so stupid, so insulting to the intelligence that if the program he was viewing were not only his favorite, he would have closed his TV set. The run of this commercial seem to be that they have to be done to exact the pound of flesh from the televiewers. Tit for tat. More tit, less tat. In other words, more commercials for less edifying programs.

He was not against the sponsoring firms getting their "pound of flesh" if that was what they wanted. What he rebelled against was the manner by which these commercials were being foisted on the viewing public. It seemed then that the sponsors were running amuck throwing those lousy commercials at the televiewers.

If these commercials were revolting, so was the TV station which always took its viewers for a ride. It was literally a ride. It would not put on a good show, schedule it for a certain time to run for a certain period. Presumably because it does not have a healthy respect for time schedules, the programs often get long drawn.

Which he considered quite unfair. He had always made it a point to listen to radio programs or to view teleplays consecutively. It happened that one program would be on another station. So he wanted that as soon as the first program is through, he would readily be able to start with the other program.

But he couldn't make his programs dovetail as he desires because of the dilatory tactic of the TV station. To him it was unfair, quite below the belt.

He confided this to Juaning during their tete-a-tete. Juaning said that the TV station couldn't perpetrate its shenanigans anymore. It seemed that this TV station discovered that it was losing sponsors because of these tactics. It had to put a brake to its bad practices. In fact, it had totally abandoned its way of programming after several bitter lessons when not only its sponsors withdrew their accounts but televiewers began shying away from the TV station.

Which made him think. There's really no substitute for commercials with integrity, or anything with integrity. They all pay in the end.

"Tonight," Juaning said, "we'll have one of the best TV shows on."

"Probably it has so many sponsors," he said.

"Well, yes," Juaning replied. "In fact it would have 20 sponsors."

"They would just take up the time of the program itself." he said.

"No," the son replied. "In fact their commercials would be made at the start of the program. You'll never see them even after the whole show is over."

"How is that again?" h asked. "The emcee usually announces: The showing of this picture is made possible by the following sponsors: Company A, manufacturer of that quality toilet soap; Company B, manufacturer of the pleasant cigarette; and other companies. . . In order to assure you of full and uninterrupted viewing and listening pleasure, our commercials are made once and only at the start of this program. Our main concern is your televiewing pleasure and convenience. The commercials and advertisements are only secondary to that. We really care that you will enjoy this program."

"I'll buy that!" Juanito almost shouted.

-o-

His son came from the kitchen after taking a drink of water. He continued, "I would like to relate to you a little story that would be a sequel to that about which we were talking just a few minutes earlier."

"What about?" h asked.

"It's about a musical program that combines good taste and artistry. The blend has an edifying effect on the viewer," Juaning replied. "There are ads too, TV ads. But these TV ads were subtle and clever but never tricky."

"I like these ads," he remarked. "They are whole and complete. They leave nothing to the imagination to dirty up. They are honest, too. They have integrity."

"Take this auto ad," he said. "You should notice its honesty. The sponsor could easily pass the car as the best of the lot. In fact he could get away with if he did just that. I know the car myself. It is really one of the best in the world. But the sponsors went out on a limb by reminding the viewers it is quite expensive owning such a car because the gasoline consumption of the high-powered engine is naturally high."

"Or this promoter ad," he continued. "The pomade could help in grooming one's hair well. The pomade has been so made that it really grooms the hair well. It has also its disadvantages, and the pomade's manufacturer have included these in the advertisement. That the pomade is a dust catcher the manufacturer did not mince any word about it. Consequently, it dirties up the hair, although only one shampoo is necessary to clean it."

"We need more of such advertisements going on our TV sets," he said.

"Yes," he replied. "We all need advertisements with integrity. The manufacturers of the products that they are foisting on us. A high pressured advertising campaign can easily hoodwink the people. But then you cannot fool all the people all the time. Sponsors should not choose that easy way. They stand to lose doing it. They should be more honest about their products. They should tell us the advantages and disadvantages of buying their products."

"If you were to ask me, father," Juaning said, "I would rather buy a poor product that has been sold honestly than a good one that has been forced on me through dishonest means. The one generates confidence while the other one makes the buyer uncertain. I also believe that we are also entitled to make our choices right. I would readily feel I had been cheated a thousand fold by buying a product about which nothing honest has been said."

"Honesty has always been the best policy," he said. "I think the sponsors should be honest about their products if they expect to acquire lasting respect for them."

"Which reminds me of George Washington story," he added. "Had Washington not been truthful when he was a boy, would he have been President of the United States?"

"I don't think so," Juaning said. "You know when one

acquires one thing at an early age, he is not able to discard it anymore. In the same analysis, a product could not grow or could not be imprinted on the minds of the people if it were sold through hoaxes."

"You have quite a point there, son," he said. "Quite a point."

All of us should try to be honest and truthful, he said to himself. If we were not honest with ourselves we would not amount to anything. We would just be fooling ourselves, and if there is anything that contribute to the downfall of any man it is not to be true to oneself. Just try fooling yourself once, he told himself. What happens? Worse things happen. You lose self-confidence, you begin to have doubts, in fact you help in losing respect of yourself. And when that happens you are gone. In the words of an American friend, you are a goner. You are not worth a whit. You become a cipher in the scheme of things.

Hence, one should be honest with himself. He should not attempt to delude himself. "To thine own self be true and thou canst be false to any man."

"Penny for your thoughts," said Juaning.

"Oh," he said, "I'm sorry, son. I was again thinking of how things would be without honesty and truthfulness. In the case of TV ads, there would be nothing to think about. Who gives TV ads without integrity a hoot?"

Yes, who gives anyone without integrity a hoot, anyway?

Chapter 19 - Conservation Of Natural Resources

After the enlightening discussion with Juaning on the loud playing of radio and TV sets and the integrity of commercials, he repaired to the kitchen where his wife was still busy doing her chores. His wife was still the beautiful woman he knew. Her face lighted up as he approached her.

"Are you going to inquire about that other wonderful meal that I am going to prepare for you?" she asked jestingly.

"Well," he said, "sort of. But I just wanted to say that you are still beautiful, that time had not changed the woman I had married."

"There you go again," she said. "Still at it? I told you that I am going to prepare a wonderful meal for you and no amount of flowery words would alter that. I doubt if your florid diction would help in making me change my mind."

"Please," he said. "Please don't change your mind."

"Now," she replied, "don't go down on your knees. You used to go down on your knees when you wanted to get something from me."

"Oh, really," he said. "Maybe I would if you don't get that meal prepared."

"By the way," he said. "What will that meal be?"

"Tonight," his wife announced, "we will feast on fish. I am going to market this afternoon and get us a tanguingue (fish)."

"It better be fresh fish or you will make me fast this evening," he said.

"It will be fresh fish and you will relish it as you never relished fish before," his wife said. "We never have known frozen fish for a long time, not that it is scarce. It is that we always have fresh fish always available."

"I hope it is not a catch due to dynamite fishing," he said.

"Our fishermen do not use dynamite anymore," his wife replied. "They had learned from the bitter lesson of the past when our fish resources became depleted by blast fishing, trawling and indiscriminate fishing."

He smiled, hoping his wife was not kidding him. He recalled the times when blast fishing was rampant. In all corners of the archipelago it was being resorted to by fishermen who come in all kinds. Good fishermen, bad fishermen, amateur fishermen, expert fishermen, big fishermen, small fishermen --they all used the easy way of catching fish by blasting, trawling, electrocuting or using poison. Fishermen get maimed or killed by blast; or people sickened by poisoned fish, but the illegal fishing went on.

And it was bad for the fish that abound in the waters of the country. Even their fry were not spared, and that was bad, for how can fish multiply without the fry? How can fish survive?

But how would fishermen know? They were all wrapped up in their self interest. Their selfishness were getting the better of them. They did not give a check to the future. They were preoccupied
with the present little knowing that such nonchalance would spell not only their doom but also the doom of their fellow countrymen.

He remembered, too, that outcry that was then raised by the responsible segments of the citizenry against illegal fishing. Statistics were waved before the eyes of the people, showing them that if they didn't take heed of these warnings they were only sealing their doom. Information on the preservation of our fish resources were disseminated throughout the country in the hope that it would help solve the critical problem facing the nation. But nobody took heed.

As a sidelight to this campaign, attention was also focused

on the denudation of our watersheds by illegal logging being made by unscrupulous wildcat lumbermen and well-entrenched businessmen in the logging enterprise. Flash floods were caused partly by denuded watersheds that could no longer hold water because they had been stripped bare of trees.

The situation was really bad for the nation. It not only reflected on national discipline but also highlighted the fact that the people were fast becoming engaged in a new form of cannibalism --they were eating themselves dead because of their irresponsibility.

But nobody really took heed of these warnings. Nobody was sane enough to tell right from wrong. The fact of the matter was that a certain national insanity was sweeping the nation at the time. It took all forms but they all boil down to the desire of the people to make money fast.

If using dynamite was illegal, the fishermen devised means to make substitutes for dynamites. And how resourceful these fishermen proved to be flaunting the law. But now his wife informs him that illegal fishing is no more. One no longer hears of fish being blasted out of the water. Neither does he hear of fish being taken out of their habitat through the use of electricity. Ditto with illegal logging.

It was his wife who finally related to him how all this came about.

A former great President of the country, by the simple expedient of an executive order, decreed that conservation would be an integrated national policy. He started right by charging the Department of Education to include teaching conservation in Education for Community Living which was already a compulsory subject in the curriculum. Our school children learned when they were young --very rightly so --to conserve water, the wood, electricity, food. They were taught how to wash dishes, not in the water-wasting way beneath an open tap, but by using wash basins. All water leaks were taboo. They were taught how to conserve fire wood and electricity used in cooking by limiting the heat once the pot begins to boil. They were taught to get only enough food on their plate which they can finish --absolutely no leftovers. They were taught why it is so necessary to conserve the fishes in our seas by catching only the adult fishes, returning to the sea all small fry. The whole nation literally went to war against dynamite fishing, and the other nefarious methods of poisoning, electrocuting and indiscriminate trawling which are the bane of the small fry and the spawn. The same crusade was waged against illegal logging and the destructive kaingin.

The net result of the conservation campaign was almost unbelievable. Every home and office had enough water to use. Because of the general education of the conservation of electricity, the thieving consumer learned it was not worthwhile to steal electricity. Power companies reduced their rates --a logical result due to increased profits. The chain reaction generated by the conservation crusade resulted in the general well being of the nation and people.

So that was what happened, he said to himself. Times indeed have changed. And times would change for the better if men only realize that there is little that they can get out of from this world should   greed   prevail   on   them.

Chapter 20 - The Taximeter

Late in the afternoon, after having had a refreshing siesta, he decided to make a round of the city just to see for himself how changed it had been. Like any other doubter, he wanted to see the evidence. So he told his wife and son that he would take a "walk" although literally walking was not his object.

Out in the street he hailed a taxi. He wanted to go to a particular place which he could not seem to recall where it was located, after the long years of absence.

"Please take me to that place," he told the taxi driver.

"If you are going to that place only, you need not take a taxi," said the drive. "Just walk straight ahead and turn left at the first corner and you are practically there."

Juanito was so overjoyed by the driver's integrity. He was speechless for a while. Then he recalled the place he wanted to see, and told the driver, "I'll see that place later, but I do want to go to other places."

As the taxi cruised along, he noticed that his taximeter was a far cry from the old taximeter that he knew. The old taximeter looked to him like an infernal machine with slits through which one could see small numbers registering the fare. He had hated the old taximeter because one oftentimes had to guess how much the fare was already. But this one is different. The slits are wide and the numbers are clear and big.

He was surprised by the new taximeter, really. The old kind of taximeter was a small ticking contraption which was more faulty than right. It was a tricky old meter. It even ran faster than the taxi those days.

He would have occasion later to discuss the taximeter with Juaning.

"They really don't go fast anymore," he told Juaning.

"Yes, of course," Juaning said. "Taximeters don't go fast these days. If it does, you will easily know because the big and clear numbers would tell you so. Even in the dead of night, when everything is dark, you will have no difficulty in telling what your fare is. You will easily know whether you have a cheat for a driver by the meter his taxi has. But the cheating driver is no more. Neither is the tricky taximeter still around. They have vanished from the local scene by virtue of a law that metes a heavy penalty on cheating drivers, taxi operators and taximeters alike."

"The law passed Congress after a tumultuous session which saw lobbyists breaking all the rules of decency just to have the legislative measure killed. But public opinion was for the law. Congress would have blackballed it but for the clamor of the people who, feeling that they were being betrayed by their own representatives, threatened not to send any of those legislators to their posts come election time. That is why we have that taximeter."

As soon as he reached his destination, he paid the driver the amount of the fare registered on the meter. He gave the driver a bill, the smallest he had on his wallet. He was a bit reluctant in doing it, knowing full well that it was a bit off the usual run of things. He had known in the past that the driver would say he had no change or he would shortchanged. But this was new breed of taxi driver.

Chapter 21 - The Hundred-Thousandth Spittoon

After a few moments on the edge of the wide sidewalk, he crossed over to the other side of the street walking between two white lanes that protected him from the onslaught of the motor vehicles. As he reached the other side he quickly noticed a man go over to one side of the sidewalk, stopped, cupped his mouth with his hand and spat. That was not the first man that he had seen during his walk who spat in that manner. There were several others who were presumably suddenly had to spew something out of their mouths or otherwise spit. And if he had to hazard a guesstimate, that probably would have been the hundred thousandth spittoon that had been used.

People now do a proper way of spiting, he thought. Many years ago, there was no rule to it. People from all walks of life never gave a thought to how they should spit. People then didn't have a sense of hygiene. They just couldn't tell what was hygienic and what was not.

Now people had learned. But how? He had been gone fifteen years, and changes had been wrought, changes for the better. The manner of spiting must be one of them.

He had also advocated a manner of spitting in the past. His way was to have the man who would spit to squat first and spit into the gutter. He had argued that this way the sputum would be confined to one place. The sputum would not scatter.

Just spitting anywhere, he believed, was quite unsanitary. But if anyone is suddenly taken to spit, he must have a way of spiting so that it won't bother other people.

For instance, if one were to spit while riding in a speeding bus, chances are that he would bother the other passengers behind him. One can just imagine the spray that the other passengers would have to catch if one would spit indiscriminately.

But bothering other people is really a minor thing compared to the other situations that spitting in a speeding bus might create. If people could kill each other over just who should be the first to pass along a narrow way, the more chances people would get at each other people's throats for spitting quite indiscriminately.

But the best way, of course, was to stop first and look for a convenient place to spit. The convenient places are many. A garbage can, a forlorn corner.

However, one didn't have to go any further if he really has sense. He can use his handkerchief. Or if he feels his handkerchief quite expensive just for spitting, he could use a piece of paper. He could spit into the paper, wrap his sputum and throw it later into the nearest trash can.

There are ways and ways of spitting properly. A hundred ways could be devised, but common sense would do.

There was one question that had assailed him when he started noticing this spitting procedures. How did these people get to be this way.

He got the answer from two boys behind whom he was walking. The two boys were discussing the current topic in their studies.

"How should one spit in the street?" one asked the other.

"How is quite simple if you had listened to our teacher this afternoon," the other replied. "He dwelt on the subject long."

"Do you mean the talk our teacher made during the HHR hour?"

"Yes, that precisely was the time when the proper way of spitting was taken up."

"I was sleepy during that part of our class work. I was not listening well."

"You were not sleepy then," the other said. "You were busy teasing the little girl in front of you. You seem to have a crush on the girl."

"Who me?" the one said. "Honest, I was sleepy."

"Oh, well," the other said. "I believe you. But I wish you had listened to the teacher. So I won't make the trouble of teaching you the procedure once again."

"Don't be selfish," the one said. "Teach it to me now."

And so the other boy proceeded to show his friend about how one should spit while in the street. He passed by the two boys who were helping each other with their school work. He passed them quite happy because he realized that they had learned much from   HHR.

Chapter 22 - The Cinema Addict or Repeater (Paulino)

On the other side of the street he saw the giant marquee the movie currently being shown. It was a star-studded movie, judging from the names of the leading movie people he had read on the marquee.

If it was, then it must be playing to standing room only. And if it was playing to SRO, then there must be a long queue outside the movie house.

There was no long line as he had expected when he came just opposite the movie theatre. In fact, there were no people milling around just to get into the movie house, unlike in the past when it would have been literally crowded that people would spill into the sidewalk to the streets.

His curiosity got the better of him so he went to the other side of the street just to investigate this seemingly rare phenomenon. What he had seen from the other side of the street was not an illusion. It actually was true. The movie was a very popular one, it had very popular stars. And many people wanted to see it. But people have to see the movie at certain times.

He learned after making a few deductions that movie houses don't get packed anymore unlike in the old days. Showings had schedules. Only a certain number of people are allowed to view one showing. Going over the number would mean a stiff fine. Hence, people no longer were packed in movie theatres.

People had to leave the movie houses after one showing. They never are allowed to stay longer than one showing. This discounts the possibility of having people seeing the movie several times for a charge of one. This amused him a lot, because he had detested people who had the "paulino" habit. He had coined the word "paulino" (addicted repeater) from the dialect "paulit" or again.

He had felt then that people should not develop the habit because it was infuriating. Some people who had seen a movie many times are wont to tell the story of the movie during its showing. He would know when the villain would get shot, when the hero would be riding in on his white steed in a flowing white robe.

He had conceded that any man has the privilege to see a movie as many times as he likes. In fact, anyone should see a movie a thousand times if he really likes it. But he should not do so in one sitting, because that way he would be irritating other people, more specially if he is one who is irrepressible. He would likely tell the synopsis of the movie before a disgusted seatmate.

According to the usher in the movie house whom he had occasion to inquire from, movie houses are not playing to SRO crowd anymore because of an ordinance passed by the city council. The ordinance decreed that only a certain number of people should be allowed during a showing. If there was to be any standing to be done, it should be done only by a handful.

When the city mayor first attempted to implement this city council ordinance, a howl was heard from the movie house operators. These people even threatened to close their theatres just to protest the ordinance. But the city mayor was firm in his implementation of the law. The law is the law and that's that.

The movie house operators had finally to relent to the wishes of the city mayor but not without having their way sort of. They were able to request the mayor that the ordinance should not be followed to the letter. Should a movie be played to SRO it should be played to SRO but to a certain limit. The movie house would not be packed like sardines. And because the mayor was himself human, he relented.

In any case, the enforcement of the SRO ordinance was a victory to the people who had expected their leaders to go by the law.

Going back to the "paulino" (addicted repeater) habit formed by the people, he was glad that something had been done to cut into its viciousness. Otherwise it could have serious repercussions.

Chapter 23 - Queuing

(Fig. XXIII.1. Form a queue and patiently await your turn to board a bus or enter a theatre. Let there be order instead of chaos. Courtesy of Bobby Elizes -artist.)

He was contemplating the traffic on the busy main street, quietly rejoicing at the orderliness of it all, when he described a long queue at the end of the street. Suddenly he was reminded of the queues he had seen in the foreign country where he had stayed. Queues formed whenever the need arose in commercial and business establishments, movie houses, public buildings --in fact, in all places where things had to be obtained in first-come first-served basis. People just automatically fall in line.

He ambled towards the queue to see what it was all about and found that the people had fallen in line to buy meat at a grocery. In fact people jostled each other, nay, even bully each other just to get to a store counter where goods in high demand were being sold.

He had decried the practice of his people in the past of almost killing each other just to be first at a store counter, a movie ticket booth, a public conveyance or anywhere. He considered it quite primitive, not to say highly uncivilized, for people to form the semblance of an unruly mob just so they could get anywhere first. It was indeed a sad commentary on the behavior of a people who would like to be known as inhabitants of well-advanced nation in the Far East.

Why couldn't they wake up to the fact that by so behaving they were only proving to observers that they hadn't gone any farther from the way of life of mountain people? He had then asked himself. Something must be done about it --and fast.

His answer to this problem was HHR. HHR could offer the remedy to this ill. But his HHR hadn't caught on then. In fact the authorities then were lukewarm to the idea.

He had left the country without knowing what had developed insofar as this problem was concerned. But now he is seeing with his own eyes that an improvement has been made --people are now forming queues. Unlike in the past they no longer jostle just to get anywhere first. They had finally realized, perhaps through the influence of HHR, the beauty of forming queues. If people would only think of others as they would more after think of themselves, they would know the benefits of doing things in an orderly way. Forming queues, for instance, is a good example.

Chapter 24 - Bus Stops

His watch told him that it was about time that he went home. He felt like going around the city a little longer but somehow he thought that he had to retrace his steps to his home. Again he wanted to take a taxi, but on second thought he decided to take a bus. At the bus stop he fell behind a queue that was then forming. People now fall in line just to board buses and jeepneys. They no longer fall on each other just to ride these conveyances. The bus stop was a concrete shed. Unlike in the past, it was not just arbitrary distance from a corner to an electric post, plastered with a wooden sign proclaiming to one and all that it was the bus stop.

"Are all these bus stops the same?" he asked the fellow behind him.

"Certainly," the kind man answered. "They are all the same since it was decreed that they should be the same."

"By the way," the man said. "Are you new here?"

"I have just arrived from abroad," he replied. "This is my first day here."

"It's no wonder then that you don't know anything much yet about these bus stops." the man said. "Well, you see, we have these bus stops after every 250 meters. The authorities had them built to insure the convenience of the riding public. It was not an spontaneous gesture of the authorities. In fact they undertook a long project study on them. They finally decided to build these bus stops after taking so many factors into consideration, paramount among them the convenience of the riding public.

"Did anybody or any group agitate for the construction of these bus stops?" he asked.

"I couldn't say," the man replied. "But somebody must have started it. At any rate, plans about these bus stops were finalized years ago by the government authorities. The local engineer's office was mobilized to implement the plans. Before we knew it the bus stops were mushrooming all over the city."

"You mean there was a proliferation of bus stops?" He asked.

"I wouldn't say proliferation," the man answered. "The word 'proliferation' connotes something that was not planned. The fact of the matter is that I should have not used the word 'mushrooming', too, because the word again connotes something that was not planned, something that just grew out of nowhere. But there are bus stops as there are people who should use them."

"I remember many years ago," he said, "that the government had also these bus stops."

"You must have been away long enough," the man said. "Those bus stops to which you are referring if seen from today's viewpoint, would appear very stupid indeed. If I remember correctly, there seemed to be no order then. They nailed signs on electric posts saying that place was a bus stop. People got confused, especially when they had one stop for buses and one stop for jeepneys. People didn't know where to go, or if they did, it took them a long time to get into the groove. But now it is different. Once you see a shed you can easily tell that it is a bus stop. Many years ago there were sheds where no public conveyances stop."

Inwardly he felt happy at the information the man had just given him on these bus stops. His people had indeed gone a long way.

Chapter 25 - Partitions In Public Seats

A big red bus came to a full stop. He noticed that it was only filled to seating capacity. Well, maybe, there were only a few passengers. The bus couldn't get any other passengers along the way.

Some ten passengers went down the bus before the bus conductress asked those who were in the bus stop to board. He noticed that the conductress was mentally counting the number of passengers going up the bus. She stopped at ten. He was the 11th man in the line. He was about to board the bus when the conductress politely told him that he should take the next bus.

"Well," he thought. He was in no hurry, so he abided with the wishes of the conductress.

Again he fell into talking with the man behind him.

"Is that really the procedure now?" he asked him.

"Yes," the man said.

"But the bus is not yet filled," he protested.

""It was filled to seating capacity," the man said.

"Do you mean to say that passengers no longer stand in buses?"

"No more. They don't stand anymore," the man aid.

The next bus came in a few minutes time. He went up with the man behind him. Inside the bus they sat beside each other. Again they picked up the skein of the conversation they cut short before going up the bus.

"How long have you been away from our country?" the man asked.

"Fifteen years to the day." he said.

"No wonder you're not abreast with the developments here." the man said.

"Yes," he said. "I still have to know more about our country after that long stay abroad."

"A lot of things have changed," the man said. Then pointing to their seats, he said: "Do you notice these partitions which are creatively designed? Probably they were not there fifteen years ago."

"Yes," he said. "Many years ago people had to sit quite close to each other, too close for comfort."

"That was precisely the reason that the Public Service Commission required bus operators and jeepney owners to have these partitions on these seats," the man said.

"Do you think the jeepneys have them too?" he asked.

"Yes," the man said, "the passenger jeepneys have them too."

"You know," said the man, "having these partitions have many advantages. It separates you from the man next to you. It gives you a seat solely for your own. It confines a passenger to his seat. For instance, a passenger no matter how big of a person he or she is could be confined to one seat without necessarily inconveniencing the other passengers. They could not just stick their legs out in the aisle. In other words, these partitions make for mutual convenience of the passengers."

"You're right," he said. "Which should be the case. Each of us should see to it that we don't make other people uncomfortable. And these partitions help much."

He remembered too, many years ago that passengers more often than not hog seats to themselves. They put things on the seats, depriving other passengers of the comfort they are looking for when they are seated in a bus or a jeepney. Some women even make their umbrellas stick out or protrude in the aisles.

But now people seemed to have learned that they should

mutually make each other comfortable, especially when they are riding public conveyances. He was about to ask his newly found friend how this came about when he found the man starting to enlighten him on the subject.

"We learned these things in grade school," the man said. "HHR."

"HHR in the schools?" he asked.

"Yes," the man said. "In college too. We were taught the subject till it almost made our ears run."

He smiled. He was happy about it.

"But it was good," the man said. "People had balked at taking the subject at first, but they soon relented when they learned of its beneficial effects. They had thought it was a form of regimentation.

Maybe. But actually it was no regimentation at all."

"It is a form of discipline," he said.

"Yes," he man said. "That's what I'm driving at. Discipline. Discipline in a big way because it has transformed the nation."

"National discipline," he said.

"Yes, really, national discipline," the man said. "Just like the one they had in Japan. I suppose it was the Japanese who started it all."

"National discipline, you mean," he said.

"Yes, of course," the man said.

"The Japanese were just one of them," he said. "There were the British and the Germans too. The British have their own form of national discipline and its beneficial effects were felt immediately after the Second World War when the empire where the sun never set was prostrate. They had their austerity. They practiced austerity as no nation practiced it. And they benefited from it too. Then there were the Germans. You can imagine how they rose from the ashes of war like the mythical phoenix."

"You seem to know more about these things," the man said.

"Well," he said, "yes."

Chapter 26 - Behavior in Public Transports

(Fig. XXVI.1. Always try to comport yourself like a truly evolved human being, considerate of others, sensitive to the conditions around you, not callous and indifferent. Courtesy of Bobby Elizes artist.)

The bus ride made him reminisce of the old days when bus or jeepney passengers abused the tolerance of their fellow passengers.

These thoughtless passengers, unmindful of the discomfiture they were causing their fellow passengers, would take their seats as if they were at home lazily lounging before a TV set, enjoying the program in spite of the inconvenience they were causing.

He clearly recalled the time he was seated beside a fellow passenger who probably thought he owned the whole jeepney. The man had his legs spread too wide and his arms were akimbo. What was worse, the man was smoking and the smoke from his cigarette was getting into his eyes. Moreover the flying embers posed a danger to barongs and nylons. Although that was not the first time that he found himself in such a situation, he considered it the worst he had experienced. At the time he was taking a long ride and the man, too was in for a long ride. So during the ride he had to sit on the edge of his seat, clinging to the slim rod which served as a handrail for dear life and limb. Although he arrived at his destination safe, he felt not so sound just because of the contumacious habit of a fellow passenger who had no regard for the comfort of another.

Then there was a time he again got seated beside a lady passenger. Because of the short skirts women were then wearing, the lady passenger had to sit sideways just to avoid putting herself into an uncompromising situation. But by the way the lady passenger had seated herself, he found himself in an uncomfortable sitting position.

There were many instances that he had suffered those rides because of the thoughtlessness of other fellow passengers, so much so that he was prompted to draw up a set of rules on how to sit in a jeepney or bus.

He had then contended that bus or jeepney passengers must sit straight while having a ride. They must so sit that they won't so much as bother the passenger sitting beside them.

He said that they should not spread their legs wide. They must put their knees together while sitting in a jeepney or bus. By spreading their legs wide, they not only make their fellow passengers uncomfortable but also demonstrate that they lack good breeding or they just had not been able to absorb the teaching of good manners in school.

Bus or jeepney passengers should see to it that they occupy only part of the seat that should be enough for them. They should not attempt to hog the whole seat for themselves.

If bus or jitney passengers are carrying things, like bundles, rods, umbrellas or what have you, they should make it a point that they don't get into the way of other passengers. Besides, bus and jeepneys are for passengers only. Bundles, bags, and other bulky items have no place in these jeepneys or buses, especially jeepneys where space is often cramped.

These are but a few of the points he wanted stressed in the set of rules he had drawn up. But how to communicate them to those concerned? How to bring them to the ken of these people?

The only course to take was to use the schools which would preach the gospel of HHR. That was the only course he could suggest. It was through the schools that these things could be channeled. But then at the time the schools were not prepared to accept his suggestions. The educational pundits were either too naïve or too enmeshed in their old rules that they couldn't take any action on his suggestions.

The changes that he was now seeing, however, had made him conclude that somehow his suggestions had sunk in. If he were to believe the man sitting beside him who earlier had talked about his HHR, his suggestions concerning the proper ways of sitting in a bus or jeepney has finally been adopted.

The Public Service Commission was awakened too. He remembered the auto-calesas (horse-dawn) of yore designed to seat two persons each side but actually jammed to seat three persons were redesigned to seat three persons conveniently by lengthening the seats and providing compulsory proper partitions between passengers.

Ah....in at least one way the government demonstrated its intention to "recognize and dignify" the Filipino workers who generally ride the jeepneys.

Chapter 27 - Safety

As the bus lumbered along the avenue, he had observed how safety was exercised by the people. At bus stops, the bus came to a full stop. It does not start again until the conductor announces that the bus would not go on its trip until every passenger had taken his seat.

Which was a far cry from the practices of the past. Many years ago drivers would run their buses or jeepneys even before the passenger had alighted or has gone up the public conveyance as the case may be. There was at the time no regard for safety. Everything was done in a daredevil manner.

Many years ago cigarette vendors and newsboys clambered up buses and jeepneys like acrobats just to sell their wares. Now he had noticed their conspicuous absence. He had an unusual feeling about the whole thing, but when he realized how much in terms of human lives had been saved from being lost in freak accidents, he instantly feel relieved.

This concern for safety by the people made him very happy indeed. He had once contended that safety awareness is the result of good human relations. A world inhabited by men who concern themselves with safety every chance they get is the creation of good human relations.

Paraphrasing Albert Schweitzer, all of us must have a reverence for life, he had once expressed. We must endeavor to preserve life at all costs, and the least expensive way of doing it is by developing habits that will not only make us live safely but also make other people live in a safe world.

One must at least gain the experience that a safe act promotes good human relations. The man who looks first to the left before crossing the street, and the driver who slows down when he comes near the street corner practice safe acts that relieves both pedestrian and motorist of certain apprehensions.

A man who is careful with his job eases tensions. A factory worker, for instance, before he goes to his job must make it a point to indulge in safe acts which in the long run would protect him from fatal errors.

On the other hand a man who does not have a regard for safety, who is a daredevil in a manner of speaking, easily becomes the bane of his neighbors, his associates and everyone who comes in contact with him. One does not feel safe when he is around.

Chapter 28 - Working Clothes

In the course of his bus ride home, he had also noted that he did not have the instance of seeing anyone riding the public conveyance in dirty working clothes. Everybody was dressed cleanly, so much so that anybody would rub elbows with them anytime.

Many years ago people didn't give a hoot whether they rode the public conveyances in clean clothes or not. They had the impression that so long as they could pay their fares, it didn't matter whether they'd have to go riding in their soiled pajamas, or in oily, smelling working clothes.

It was truly discomfiting to be seated in a bus or jeepney with a man who had just come from a hard day's work smelling of sweat and the sun and wearing the clothes that he had worked with. More so if one was dressed up and was on the way to attend an important conference or party. He would no doubt be contaminated with the ill-smell of which his seatmate exudes.

If companies would only provide proper wash rooms and then require their employees, especially those engaged in menial tasks to come to work and from work dressed properly, the problems of people going around in their dirty working clothes would be solved. But then it would take more than company regulations to make these people, particularly day laborers, stevedores, and the like to follow such a rule. Somehow some sort of a slow process should be applied to drive home the point into the heads of these lowly workers.

Because they couldn't be sent back to school anymore, he had proposed that these people should be made to attend short seminars that would help them absorb some fundamentals on HHR. A short course on harmonious human relations would help in awakening them to the fact that there are things that they should do and should not do, things that they have to practice daily, specific acts that they have to do.

In this case the specific act is to make them understand the benefits that could be derived from coming to work and going home in clean clothes, not their dirty working clothes. They should be made to feel the full impact of how one's personality could be enhanced if he should be coming to work and going home in clean clothes.

This education in the specific act should be a continuing one. It should not be taken up in the 'ningas cogon' (quick grass burning) way. It should be pounded into the heads of these lowly workers again and again to make it a part of their daily norm of conduct.

Deducing from what he had observed and the possible motivations behind it, he concluded that perhaps his idea introducing the HHR into the mainstream of consciousness of the people might have helped in developing the specific act of coming to work and going home in clean clothes in the people.

Again he felt acquitted by what he had observed. Somehow, he thought, the things that he had envisioned his HHR would do had finally been realized.

Chapter 29 -Tolerance

At the rate the bus was going which was 40 KPH, he calculated that it would require half an hour for him to reach home. In the meantime, he made a review of what he had done many years ago, and foremost in his mind then was the piece about intolerance and how it served as a deteriorating factor in human relations.

He had just observed that with a modicum of tolerance people could live together harmoniously, short of saying that they could co-exist no matter what their ideologies, beliefs, creeds, stations in life and the like. They could work together, forgiving each other's shortcomings and making up for what the other fellow lacked. And this gave him the opportunity to recall to mind that piece he had written about tolerance.

"Tolerance," he had then written, "is the ability to understand another person's opinions and actions without accepting them or changing one's own. Whenever I am tempted to be critical of another's opinion or action, I always think of a Chinaman's answer to someone who asked him: 'Why do you bring food to the graves of your dead when they cannot eat them?' To which question the Chinaman smilingly answered: 'For the same reason that you bring flowers to the graves of your dead even if they cannot smell them.'"

According to him, the spirit of tolerance is one of the

underlying and basic tenets of democracy. Volumes have been written and will yet to be written, he had argued, on tolerance, eloquent orations and speeches have been delivered and will yet be delivered cajoling men to tolerance, but no finer tribute could be made to it than Voltaire who had said: "I disagree in what you say but I will defend to the death your right to say it."

If a man can disagree in what his neighbor says but allows his neighbor to say it nevertheless, he said, even without going to the extent of defending to the death the right to say it, democratic living and harmonious human relations are assured to be with us for a long time to come. Presidential candidates may then campaign in any nook and corner of the land without the need of bodyguards.

He rejoiced in what Helen Keller had said about tolerance and he often quoted the statement just to drive home the point he would like to make concerning the subject. The quotation is, to wit:

"The highest result of education is tolerance. Long ago men fought and died for their faith; but it took ages to teach them the other kind of courage --the courage to recognize the faiths of their brethren and their rights of conscience. Tolerance is the first principle of community; it is the spirit which conserves the best that all men think. No loss by flood and lightning, no destruction of cities and temples by the hostile forces of nature has deprived men of so many noble lives and impulses as those which intolerance has destroyed."

It was a beautiful quotation and he had made it a guide in his appreciation of tolerance as a subject.

He had also occasion to talk about one's tolerance of the other's religion. He said: Those who are tempted to be critical of their neighbor's religion must be reminded that miracles happen everywhere in this earth. Not any place or religion can claim monopoly of miracles --God's rewards to sincere prayers and spontaneous demonstrations of faith, proving beyond any doubt that all men are the children of God, whatever the race, color or creed.

So he had proposed that every child should be taught early in life to believe in his religion, that his religion is the true religion, and that he has also to respect his neighbor's religion and in his absolute right to believe in it. Then quoting Lecomte Du Novy, the famous scientist and author, who said: "True religion is in the heart; the rite is only a pretext."

He said that there are several forms of tolerance that should be ever present in the hearts of true men and they are according to Paul Turney, Grand Master of Masons, whom he quoted:

1   It is that BROADMINDEDNESS which both prompts and enables a man to regard every other man as his peer, and entitled equally with himself to his individual opinions and sentiments

regarding matters political, philosophical, and religious.

2   It is that SPIRIT OF UNSELFISHNESS which leads a man to recognize that each person sees things from his own point of view, and to admit that it is always possible for himself to be wrong and the other to be right.

3   It is that KINDNESS OF THOUGHT which prompts a man to respect the opinions of his fellows as if someday they might be his own.

4   It is that CHARITABLE JUDGMENT upon the actions, the conduct, and even the foibles of others which each man wish passed upon his own, and which concedes that another man may be honest at heart even though mistaken as wrong in his opinion or conclusion.

But one of the ugliest forms of intolerance is tyranny. He said that tyranny has been the cause of many of the world's wars. History tells us, he said, that no tyranny has ever triumphed in the end because free men always succeeded to smash the forces of tyranny.

If he had his way he would have the spirit of tyranny killed early in the young people by instilling in them the words of Lincoln who said: "No man is good enough to govern another man without the latter's consent."

Chapter 30 - Holidays

Again he looked at his watch. It was the second time in the day when he looked at his watch, a gesture which amazed him a little. It was not his habit to look at his watch. In fact he hadn't bothered to keep time but in as much as a watch is a fetish as it is a status symbol, he had worn a watch.

He was wearing a special watch. It was not only telling the time. It was also telling the date and the day. It was a Thursday according to the watch.

He was preoccupied with his watch that he forgot to get off at the last bus stop, but it was more than a blessing because at the next bus stop there was a magazine stand about which he browsed for a time. He looked over what were selling and finally bought a newspaper.

He scanned the newspaper before he started for home. A two-column head in the front page announced that the next day was a holiday. The nation was observing the death anniversary of a national hero, which called for the special holiday.

At home he got to talking to Juaning about the coming holiday. As they were talking, his eyes fell on the wall calendar and leafed through it.

"Aside from the legal holidays that we have, son," he said, "there are also in the list a number of special holidays. Are these special holidays already being equated with legal holidays?"

"No, father." said Juaning. "It just happens that the President of the Republic has already issued an executive order in advance designing certain special holidays."

"How and why?" he asked.

"Why and how should be the sequence of this thing?" Juaning said. "The highest magistrate of the land, the chief executive, in fact all our chief executives, have learned that it would be much better for the people to know when there would be special holidays in advance in order to prepare them well for spending the holiday. They had believed that a holiday which is badly spent because of lack of planning is no holiday at all. Hence, our chief executives decided to declare special holidays in advance. With the exception of very special holidays, like a day after a calamity, or a day when a very important person, a foreign dignitary, for instance, who deserves a national welcome, all special holidays are declared in advance."

"A special study committee of the office of the President handles this matter. It is responsible for the determination of the holidays that are to be declared and giving the proper recommendation to the chief executive for proclamation."

"The committee ruled: If we must have holidays, people should derive the maximum benefits there from. A holiday, with the only possible exception of the New Year, shall never be sandwiched between working days, and shall be observed on the nearest Monday or Friday."

"When a holiday falls on a day sandwiched between working days, what is the reaction of intelligent people? Stupid thing to do, and should be corrected. If we must have a holiday, let us derive maximum benefit and enjoyment out of it by observing it on a day adjacent to another non-working day so there will a group of two, three or four days together available to undertake that trip one has been planning to do all these years, the project to add or alter that part of the house, to redo the painting, make the cabinet or transfer the garage. A holiday must perforce be observed on the nearest Monday or Friday, granting Saturday at long last, becomes universally a non-working day, so one can look forward to a long week end of three glorious days in a row. Also, the President should declare a holiday well in advance, with very few exceptions, so one can plan with plenty of time ahead how to profitably derive the maximum benefit and enjoyment out of the holiday. Another point is that part of the enjoyment of the holiday comes from the thought and anticipation that holidays are coming. Why deny a hard-working man and busy housewife such pleasures of anticipation."

"Any construction or shop superintendent or foreman who handles workmen knows that a working day sandwiched between holidays is not a day where he can expect a high degree of efficiency from his men."

"Unless it is impossible, most holidays are made to fall on a Monday. The reason for this is that it is much better to link a holiday with Sunday which is a day of rest or the working world than having to make it fall on any other day. Of course, it often is also made to fall on a Friday, because it amounts to the same thing. And this has proven advantageous to the working people. They more or less are spared the effort to harbor the tired thought that they would be spending a holiday which they cannot enjoy."

"Was this idea really the original idea of our chief executives?" he asked.

"Not quite," Juaning replied. "If I am not mistaken, it was a foreign writer who put the idea in the minds of our people who in turn broached the idea to the office of the chief executive. At first it was not given a thought because the initial proposal had the earmarks of a crank suggestion. But as more people talked and wrote about it, the office of the President sat up and noticed. It was then that plans were drawn up and given to the President for approval."

"A good thing more often than not draws undue criticism, just as a tree heavy with fruit is stoned by passersby who covet the fruits. This very same thing happened to this good measure. Certain sectors put up objections. The main argument against it was voiced by the businessmen who thought it would adversely affect the smooth flow of work in their respective establishments and their business communities. This argument was however torn to pieces by a counter argument penned by a respected and prominent member of the community who himself was also a businessman. It didn't take the President long to adopt the proposal."

"Yes," he said, "the declaration of these holidays has its merits."

"It has," Juaning replied. "There was a time, not so long ago, when a certain chief executive almost ran amuck declaring holidays left and right. If it suited his whim or the whims of those who were close to him, a holiday was declared. The President who followed after him corrected this however. He did it by not declaring a holiday unless it was very necessary. Eventually the plan evolved. Now we have this plan."

"Wonderful," he said. "Wonderful."

Chapter 31 - Punish Water Wasters

He had not aged a day yet at home when he observed so many changes, among them how his family used water. He had been intrigued by the way his son avoided using water if he could use something else. He was also amused at his wife who seldom took to water like a duck as he used to say to her during early years back. Both his wife and his son seemed to have reduced their time taking showers at a minimum. They did not take long in the bathroom.

Many years ago, he remembered, whenever Juaning would take a bath, he would hear the rush of water in the bathroom. He noted when his son took a shower after he came, he did not hear the familiar rushing of the water.

When they sat down to take their supper, he inquired rather naively if both of them had cultivated an abhorrence for water when he was away. He explained his query by citing the instances he had observed.

"No, father," said his wife. "We love water so much that given the chance to hoard it we would do so at the least provocation."

"Why then do you seem to avoid getting contact with water?"

"Oh, forgive us, father," it was Juaning who cut in the conversation.

"Forgive us if we looked strange to you trying to 'avoid' water as you say. It's not that we don't use the water as it used to be. We have to use water in such a way so that we won't be wasting it."

"That's noble of you two." he said. "We really should not be wasting water. We are lucky we have we have enough water to go by in this country. In other countries, particularly in the foreign country where I stayed, where water is scarce, leading the life we lead is quite difficult. Some countries even go to the extent of putting their people on half rations insofar as water is concerned. That's how precious water is in those countries."

"But aren't you exaggerating your role in this conservation of water by the way you are using it?" he asked.

"On the contrary, father," Juaning replied. "We are not exaggerating our actions. You see, we have deferred in informing you that water wasters in our country are now being punished under the Water Law."

"Water Law?" he asked. "What's the law about?"

"It is all about the use of water," his wife said. "According to the section of the Water Law, people caught wasting water face a fine of P500 or 30 days imprisonment or both."

"How does the law enforcement agencies catch violators of the law? Do they attach special meters to residences of water consumers?"

"Of course not," the wife countered. " We still have the same old water meters. They have not been changed."

"How then is the law enforced?" he asked.

"Well, there seems to be no use for enforcing the law anymore," his wife said. "The people had learned through experience not to waste water."

Then the wife recounted how the people regimented themselves into not wasting water. "There was a time when water was aplenty. People used the water wantonly. They did not seem concerned whether or not the water was being used wisely. They even allowed their faucets to leak."

"Then the unexpected happened. The denuded water sheds stopped yielding enough water to meet the needs of the people. Rivers, creeks, and waterways began showing signs of drying up. Water shortage became a daily occurrence especially in the urban areas. Water, for the first time in our history, became a problem."

"It was at this point that the leaders in our country stepped in. Alarmed by the increasing demand for water and the shortage of water supply, they began looking for remedies one of which was the passage of the Water Law. But the law itself did not suffice as a remedy. Civic organizations all over the land started impressing into the minds of the people the importance of conserving water. This campaign brought forth results which almost made the wastage of water rare even without the benefit of applying the Water Law."

"That's why we use water only when the necessity arises," his wife concluded. "And we use water as if every drop is as precious as its equal volume in gold."

"I'm glad you have told me that story," he said. "Now I'll know how to use water. I don't want to land in jail because I violated the Water Law."

Chapter 32 - Latrines

After supper, he stood at the veranda of their house, a **vantage point** in their house where there was a commanding view of the neighborhood from where it stood and he could see whatever his neighbors were doing in the street. Many years ago at these hours he was witness to the unpleasant rituals engaged in by his neighbors due to extreme necessity. At the time he saw his neighbors squat behind make shift sheds to defecate because they were either too lazy to dig latrines or too poor to afford themselves with midden sheds.

Too, at these hours many years ago, he had seen some of his neighbors throw paper bags full of wrapped excreta in the streets, if they cared to walk a little, or from windows, if they didn't feel like going down their houses. The shamelessness had appalled him. Had his neighbors gone so callous that they have decided to imperil the health of the people around them with their thoughtlessness? Is there hope that they would change their ways?

Those were the question that assailed his mind then. Until he left the country the questions remained unanswered.

At the time, during moments of meditation, he had debated with himself on the merits of going to his neighbors and telling them in the face that what they do were wrong. He would shoot off his mouth, spew out statistics on the mortality of people who are ignorant of the elementary laws of sanitation and inspire fear for disease on them with the end in view of rousing them into meeting their responsibilities. But more often than not he found himself hesitating to carry this out. He was afraid that he might be ridiculed for his attempt. He might be accused of preaching like an unfrocked priest. So he let his idea go but he wished his neighbors would become enlightened.

Had his neighbors changed?

That was what he wanted to know as he stood at the verandah waiting for an event that would disprove his expectations. When he thought the vigil enough he finally decided to go down to inquire from his neighbors what had made the change. He wanted to know what the reasons were. And he would know this by going down the house, making a round of the neighborhood and baiting his neighbors to talk about the change.

"We had to dig latrines because our children insisted," said Mang Ambo, a sixtyish man who lived a few houses from his residence. "We were told by visiting teachers that if we persisted in perpetuating the practice of defecating in that area we would stink to high heavens and be in danger of getting sick."

"We took up the matters in a meeting of our neighborhood association," said Mang Pepe. "All were agreed on banishing the stink but everybody just didn't know how. One of us suggested that we see the local authorities and solicit their help. It was a good idea so we created a committee to make representations."

"The local government was at first lukewarm to our request.

When we threatened to bring the matter to a national agency they reconsidered," said Tata Pendong.

"The assistance which the local government extended was in the form of an expert. The expert taught the people about hygiene, then went down to brass tacks. Because the local government didn't have enough funds to finance an extensive midden shed project, it prodded the neighborhood to tackle the matter from the point of view of self-help. There were cries of disappointment at first, but as negotiations on the matter progressed, the neighborhood decided to go along with the local government's proposal. Hence, there is now a latrine for every home."

Satisfied with his findings, he returned home, his heart almost leaping in jubilation at the observations he had made. Things are much better now than when le left. Everybody seemed proficient now in looking for that unknown, the "x" in human behavior.

Chapter 33 - Planned Parenthood

A few minutes after he had gone up the house, his son came in, looking dressed as a mannequin in the window. It developed that Juaning had just come from a visit to his sweetheart who lived out of the city, and from the joy that he saw written in the boy's face he was certain that he had some news to blurt out.

"You know, father," Juaning said, "I got news for you. My sweetheart Vinning is happy that you are here now. She is extending her regards."

"Do I know her?" he asked. "Have we known their family?"

"No," Juaning said. "I met Vinning in college. She's a pretty girl, comes from a good family, works for a government agency and does well in whatever she does. I am very proud of her."

"That's nice," He said. "I suppose you have plans to get married."

"That was what I was about to tell you, father," Juaning said. "We're planning to get married."

"No objections," he said. "What does your mother say?"

"Say," he said, "there seems to be some conspiracy around here."

"CIA, Interpol, NBI?" said his wife jokingly. "No conspiracy, really. Nothing but the old, old way of giving the newcomer a big surprise."

"So you know this all along?" he asked.

"But of course," said his wife "I've been in on the secret since the two of them made it into one."

"Well, what can I say about that?" he said. "What can I say, indeed?"

"Do you mean to say that you're all for it, father?" Juaning asked.

"Yes, son," he said. "I'm all for it. When is the wedding, the long table, so to say?"

"Not far off," Juaning said. "We'll tell you when we're all set. In the meantime I suppose I ought to tell you that one of our plans is to have several children. A dozen, perhaps. Cheaper by the dozen."

"That's quite an ambitious plan." he said.

"Too ambitious indeed," Juaning said, "I really don't know if it is going to get off the launching pad."

"That's too easy," he said. "It's too easy to produce babies."

"I was only kidding about those dozen babies, father," Juaning said. "I really don't know how to face up with the problem. I doubt if I can solve it, but I'll try my best. We have this family planning idea being propagated by some groups. I suppose it would help. These groups had started this thing a long time ago. Their ideas are already catching on, but you know they're not quite extensive yet."

"Many years ago," Juaning said, "there were certain misconceptions about this family planning affairs. Many had asked whether it is a form of abortion. But of course, it is not abortion. Family planning is a safe method taught to fathers and mothers who want to limit and space pregnancies without resorting to abortion acts."

He, too, had ideas about family planning. He had once wrote to a magazine writer who unfortunately failed to get his point in this wise:

"Do you believe that 'voluntary motherhood' is the inherent right of every married woman? But of course. It is an inherent right, not an absolute right, and it is subject to certain limitations. Many of our women want to enjoy this right. But many of them do not know how. They need help."

"It is common knowledge that there is a population explosion in our country. Our country need to stabilize or check this explosion. Our leaders have to. It is a grave pressing problem, one that we couldn't just dismiss with a shrug of the shoulder."

"But we should realize," he had argued, "that we need family planning more than any other nation in the world needs it. We need the method to stabilize our population."

"Let's talk of it from the point of view of economics. Our country's gross national product is steadily going up. But our gains per capita is stagnant. Our gains are being whittled down or negated by the too rapid population increase. We seem to be a virile country. Two babies are born every minute."

"Because of our run-away population growth capital formation in our country is slow. Wage earners do not have enough to save because they have so many children to feed, to work for."

"Malthus in his Essay on Population had contended that it is necessary to regulate the growth of population and suggested that this regulation be done by the postponement of marriage and continence. Since late marriages and continence are very impractical solutions to the problem, planned or responsible parenthood could only be the answer."

But family planning then was not quite as accepted as it is now. At the time it had taken the brunt of attacks from several quarters. Nevertheless the battle for family planning went on. Most pro-vocal on family planning methods were journalists, women journalists at that, who had written pieces on family planning. One woman writer, Mary R. Tagle, wrote in this wise:

"Sometimes lost in the maze of arguments --pro and con, apropos and gratuitous --on birth control is that aside from the consideration of the mother's health and well-being is the far greater consideration, which is the ability of the parents or, in their default, the ability of the state, to provide for the necessities for proper health and education for the development of an exemplary citizen."

"Otherwise, if there is no conscious plan or restraint in the number of members of the family, more millions of underfed, uneducated, individuals will be born who will be condemned to probably even lower income and social classes than their fathers before them."

"The existence of this needy mass provides a built-in insurance for politicians who flourish by the existence of this needy mass, and the bigger and needier this mass is, the more easily they are manipulated by power and money-seeking politicians who stay in power for generations, who even distribute elements of state power among the members of the family even within the same generation."

But it was the wife of the President of the Philippines who gave the idea impetus in this country. At a gathering Mrs. Marcos indicated her acceptance of the idea for a family planning program in the country.

According to a report, she even went farther than mere acceptance. She indicated that she was willing to support such a movement, "to throw the whole weight of her public figure behind the movement."

Recent surveys conducted here confirmed findings abroad that poorer, less educated families tend to have more children than those where either or both parents are professionals earning high incomes.

The need is urgent for educating the masses on family planning especially in homes where irresponsible parenthood has bred nothing but poverty and misery.

Family planning programs have already been set up by prestigious institutions in the country. Among them is a catholic university hospital and the health department of the City of Manila.

Manila's city health planning program copied the London project with some modifications. The London project helps couples on the rhythm method with the aid of a thermometer and a chart designed to simplify the reading of the thermometer.

He had written that the country was already feeling the effects of over population in many towns and cities in the form of inadequacy of essential services such as water, light and power, transportation and others. As one congressman bewailed, "we are producing school children at a faster rate than we can build school houses to accommodate them!"

To my mind, he had said, we have to start now stabilizing our population growth and not wait for the time when we have to be frantic about it, as in Japan where sterilizations, contraceptives and legal abortions have to be resorted to as last ditch measures. At the outset let it be understood by all and sundry that birth control does not necessarily mean stopping procreation, but only limiting and properly spacing childbirths. Instead of using doubtful and expensive contraceptives and resorting to the highly immoral sterilization and abortion, "there is available a natural method of birth control, highly approved by medical science as effective, which violates no law of nature or of the author of nature." This is the so-called rhythm method.

Again he has repeatedly drove home the point that our gross national product has increased admirably during the years. Because of increased use of machines in our farms, irrigation, fertilizer in agriculture, our farm production has gone up. The growth of our factories is comparable to that of other similar developing countries. Alas, however, our gross national product per capita is almost stagnant. The reason is quite obvious.

By advocating stabilization of population growth, he does not in the least advocate let-up in increasing our economic production. Let us strive to double, treble, or expand our present production. But at the same time let us learn to stabilize our run-away population growth.

Chapter 34 - Summing up

It was one of the longest days he had spent in his life and he was sad because it was ending. He felt he had not seen everything yet, heard everything that he should hear, feel, experience and take into his bosom everything around him But then there was still another day, there was still tomorrow that he could spend or what he had missed today.

Alone in the silence of his room he came to the realization that nothing was really better than to stay home and do what one could do within his and country's resources. Running away from realities was futile. One had to face the facts or be branded a coward.

He now believed that he was more of a coward when he left the country because of his frustrations on the pretext of seeking greener pastures abroad. There really were no greener pastures, no field to graze to his heart's content. Things may look better on that side from this side, but it really was better here than anywhere else.

Had I not gone away, he told himself, I might not be just what I am now. Things were really not so bad then. It just so happened that I got singed, nay, burned by the things I had noted then.

This is the age of 'unahan' (cutting in line), 'gulangan' (cheating) and 'lamangan' (bullying or brute force), he recalled a magazine editor wrote of the times. One had to be 'swapang' (scallawag) to get ahead. It was evident in the way people take their rides in jeepneys, or board the buses during rush hours. They seemed to have no regard for the next man, for the other fellow, and if that next man, that other fellow were easy to bulldoze, sorry for him.

This type of behavior was carried over to the higher strata of life in the country. In government, officials and employees were almost killing each other, physically and morally, trying to jockey for positions. The erosive spirit of 'unahan', 'gulangan' and 'lamangan' persisted. People were stabbing each other in the back so they could get what they want. As if to complete the picture, those who are not 'swapang' were afflicted by the 'Aguinaldo' (gift) or 'gimme' (pandering) disease.

Perhaps because he was one of weak stomach, one who couldn't take it anymore, he had to leave, little realizing that what he would do would one day be counted against him. Although he could chalk it to experience, he felt it more of a bad excuse rather than anything else.

For something could be done and had already been done. He had seen the proofs earlier in the day, and he was glad he discovered that some of his ideas had helped much. He knew too well that if some reformation were to be undertaken, if any correction were to be made, it had to start in the schools. Then this could be carried over other venues, places where people could be reached in numbers. Neighborhood meetings, office seminars, congregations, radio, TV, even in movie houses. People are always willing to learn and they are always changing for the better.

There was really no need of going out of one's country to better one's lot. Most, if not all, who join the exodus to other lands in search for what they term as greener pastures are actually deluding themselves. There's really no gold at that end of the rainbow. Gold is where one finds it, and one could find it at his very doorsteps in his country.

I think I have committed a grievous mistake getting out of the country at that time, he told his wife as they were about to sleep. "How's that again?" his wife asked.

"I was thinking," he said. "Had I stayed here I might have been able to do greater things that we could enjoy together."

"Are you trying to say that 'nasa huli ang pagsisisi'? (remorse is at the end)," his wife asked.

"If you want to put it that way, yes," he said. "But then. . ."

"Do you have other excuses?" his wife asked.

"Nothing," he said. "Really nothing. However, I could not help but recall Edmund Burke when he said: 'The only thing necessary for the triumph of evil is for good men to do nothing.' Doing nothing is the same as leaving the country. Although I emulated the Christophers who said, 'Better light a candle than curse the darkness,' nothing happened."

His wife kissed his cheeks.

"Good night, father," she said.

"God night,' he replied.

Book List - Contact: job_elizes@yahoo.com - tatay@usa.com

Writings 1 Book, 2012. Updated + +

1. Obit, *Bambi Harper* + + 2. Speech, UP, 2003, *Butch Jimenez* + + 3. Speech, Silliman U, 2006, *Butch Jimenez* + + 4. The Mission Moment, *Dr. Phil Stack* + + 5. Subanon Spirits of Rice & Land - *Noel Cornel Alegre* + + 6. I Look Out The Window - *Atty. Toto Causing* + + 7. Ride On A Bus, Poem, *Melanie Ferrer, et al* + + 8. Why Am I Doing This, *Susie Barbieri* + 9. How To Court A Philippine Lady, *Rodel Ramos, et al* + + 10. Story of Bacna Surgical Mission, *Sylvia Salvador* + + 11. Catch That Story, *Tatay Jobo Elizes*

Writings 2 Book, 2012, Updated + +

1. There Is Hope For The Philippines, *Grace Padaca* + + 2. Pointers On Employment Abroad, *Melanie Aquino* + + 3. Without KNCHS: (Love story), *Atty. Toto Causing* + + 4. 422 Years Ago, *Rodel Rodis* + + 5. Filipino American History Month, *Rodel Rodis* + + 6. A Need For Reflection, Gloom, *Cesar Torres* + + 7. Did Ninoy Die For Nothing, *Joey Concepcion* + + 8. Criteria - American Institute of Philanthropy, *Charity Guidelines (Feature)* + + 9. Coming Revolution In The Ballot, *Cesar Lumba* + + 10. 2009, A Retrospective, *Cesar Lumba* + + 11. Strangers In Our Own Country, *Casiano Mayor Jr.* + + 12. The Gypsy Soul, *Casiano Mayor Jr.* + + 13. An End To Cheating, *Sonny Coloma* + + 14. Toward Culture of Giving, Not Having, *Sonny Coloma* + + 15. 100 Reasons to be Proud as Pinoys, *Anonymous*

Writings 3A Book, 2012, Updated + +

1. EPIC25, Emerging Philippines Investors Coalition, *Norman Madrid* + + 2. Management Ability As An Issue, *Dr. Rene B. Azurin* + + 3. Do We Really Want To Give Our Politicos More Power, *Dr. Rene B. Azurin* + + 4. Will 2010 Fulfill High Hopes For Better Life, *Ernie D. Delfin* + + 5. Comelec Is The Root Of All Evils, *Toto Causing* + + 6. Advantages of Federalism / Parliamentary, *Dr. Jose Abueva* + + 7. Sometimes A Great Nation, *Mar-Vic Cagurangan* + + 8. Great Conspiracy, *Mar-Vic Cagurangan* + + 9. Of Speech & Life's Riddles, *Casiano Mayor* + + 10. Bad Start To The Year, *Rod Garcia* + + 11. A Dinner Out, *Rod Garcia* + + 12. One More Time, *Roy Gaane* + + 13. Strange Noises, *Tatay Jobo Elizes* + +

Writings 3B, 2012, Updated + +

1. The Reeds & Beams, etc, + + 2. Memories+ + 3. Blowout+ + 4. Dream on + + 5. O Naraniag + + 6. Candelaria + + 7. Four P's. .+ + All 1-7 by *Ceres Busa* from her Musings + + 8 On Being Filipino-American + + 9 The Monterey Peninsula + + 10. The Salaza Fiesta+ + 11. Salawikain + + 12. Musikero + + *All 8-12 by John Reyes* + + 13. Did You Know Collections of Tidbits up to 17, all 13-17 *by Bert Guiang*+ + 14. Sharing Trivia, *Bert Guiang* + +

Writings 4A, 2012 Updated + +

1. The State of Our Nation and Democracy In 2010: Building 'The Good Society" We Want, *Dr. Jose V. Abueva* + + 2. Assessing Expanded Role of AFP in Nation Building, *Col.Dennis Acop, Ret.* + + 3. Assessing RP's Security Strategies Alternative Views, *Col. Dennis Acop, Ret.* + + 4. The Way We Were, *Fred Natividad* + + 5. Veterans of Ipo Dam, A Fiction, *Fred Natividad* + + 6. A Plea, *Miguel Reyes Reynaldo* + + 7. Int'l Youth Bowling, Berlin, My Impressions, *Marjorie Ann Elizes Reyes* + + 8. Hongkong Gold Medal in Bowling, *Marjorie Elizes Reyes* + + 9. Beijing Impressions, Youth Bowling Tournament, *Marjorie Elizes Reyes* + +

Writings 4B Book, 2012 Updated + +

1. Mi Ultimo Adios, *Dr. Jose P. Rizal* + + 2. Pag-ibig Sa Tinubuang Bayan - *Andres Bonicafio* + + 3. Reunion of Filipinos in Heaven (A Dramatic Play) - *Irineo P. Goce* - + +

4. The Forgery of the Rizal Retraction - *Irineo Goce* - + + 5. **Malas Na Bayang Pilipinas** - *Irineo Goce* - + +

Writings 5 Book - "Best Hopes" 2010, About President P-Noy + +

I. The Challenge of a Hundred Days: Believing that Filipinos can, *Tony Meloto* + + II. The 2006 Ramon Magsaysay Award for Community Service, *for Tony Meloto* + + III. Open Letter to Noynoy, *F. Sionil Jose* + + IV. A History of Pain, *Juan L. Mercado* + + V. An Open Letter to Noynoy, *From OFWS* + + VI. Pursuit of Good Governance Advocacies, *Marcelo Tecson* + + VII. A Fervent Prayer for Peace, *Cesar Torres* + + VIII. A History of Betrayal, *Perry Diaz* + + IX. Corona's Thorny Crown, *Perry Diaz* + + X. Dawn of a New Era, *Perry Diaz* + + XI. Of Mice, Boys and Men, *Philip S. Chua, MD* + + XII. A Hopeful Tomorrow - A Balikbayan Insight, *Philip S. Chua, MD* + + XIII. Global Filipinos: A Sleeping Giant, *Philip S. Chua, MD* + + XIV. Heart to Heart - Winds of Change, *Philip S. Chua, MD* + + XV. Growing Old is a Privilege, *Philip S. Chua, MD* + + XVI. Our Cruelty to Mother Earth, *Philip S. Chua, MD* + + XVII. Advice to Grads: "Never Choose Your Heroes Lightly", *Ernie Delfin* + + XVIII. Gawad Kalinga, A Progressive Movement, *Ernie Delfin* + + XIX. Why a Man Must Save and Invest, *Ernie Delfin* + + XX. Beautiful San Francisco, Pinoy Heaven, *Ted Laguatan* + + XXI. The next President and PAMUSA, *Frank Wenceslao* + + XXII. Philippne Budget Deficit, *Frank Wenceslao* + + XXIII. Money Laundering: US Tools vs. Corruption, *Frank Wenceslao* + + XXIV. Amid the Fighting, Clan Rules Maguindanao, *Jaileen F. Jimeno* + + XXV. Why I Publish Writings, *Tatay Jobo Elizes* + + +

Writings 6 Book, 2010 + +

I. SONA, State Of Nation Address, English, *Pres. Benigno Aquino III* + + II. SONA, State of Nation Address, Pilipino, *Pres. Benigno Aquino III* + + III. First 100 Days Speech, Pilipino, *Pres. Benigno Aquino III* + + IV. Finally, Another Ramon Magsaysay In The Making, *Bert Guiang.* + + V. A Covenant With Our President, *Tony Meloto* + + VI. From A Grateful Heart, A Thank You Letter, *Tony Meloto* + + VII. The Scent of Hope For The Global Filipino, *Tony Meloto* + + VIII. Fleshing Out The Broad Strokes, *Felicito (Tong) C. Payumo* + + IX. In Search Of Leaders (Part1), *Felicito (Tong) C. Payumo* + + X. In Search of Leaders (Part 2), *Felicito (Tong) C. Payumo* + + XI. A Conspiracy of Dunces, *Cesar Lumba* + + XII. Only Science Can Solve Poverty, *Flor Lacanilao* + + XIII. Education Reform Amid Scarcity, *Flor Lacanilao* + + XIV. Highblood: Obituaries/Reasons, *Flor Lacanilao* + + XV. How Money Works, *Edmund Lao* + XVI. State of Economy & Society, 2002, *Juan Dela Cruz (Txtmania)* + + XVII. Global Filipinos, *Juan Dela Cruz (Txtmania)* + + XVIII. Understanding Poverty, *Juan Dla Cruz (Txtmania)* + + XIX. Kuyakuy, *Dr. Ramon Marquez* + + XX. Cambodian Octopus, *Joey Jamito* + + XXI. Inspite Of Herself, I Still Love The Philippines, *Joey Jamito* + + XXII. Love Has Wings, *Percy Campoamor Cruz* + + XXIII. Walk For Kris, *Rod Garcia* + + XXIV. Coldblooded, But Alive, *Rod Garcia* + + XXV. It Takes A Village, *Rod Garcia* + + XXVI. Beauty Contest, *Rod Garcia* + + XXVII. Eight Points In Enlightening The Elites, *Orion Perez Dumdum* + + XXVIII. Case Against "Cellphone Revolution", *Sarah Raymundo*

Writings 7 Book, 2010 - My Vintage Pics (Biographical) Tatay Jobo Elizes

Writings 8 Book, 2010 + +

I. The Church and the State: In Search of Common Ground, *Gel Santos Relos* + + II. President Aquino: "Walang Kaibigan, Walang Kamag-anak", *Gel Santos Relos* + + III. What Makes Us "Pinoy", *Gel Santos Relos* + + IV. Minsan May Isang Puta (2007), *Mike Portes* + + V. Build Our Dream, *Jose Ma. Montelibano* + + VI. Hope In Europe, *Tony Meloto* + + VII. Wealth in Canada, *Tony Meloto* + + VIII. Parenthood: A Sacred Covenant, *Philip S. Chua* + + IX. Are We, Humans, Really Civilize? (Or, are we for the birds.), *Philip S.*

Writings 9 Book, April 2011 + +

Writings 10 Book, July, 2011 + +

18. Heart to Heart, Violence on Television, *Philip S. Chua* + + 19. Heart to Heart, Attitude Impacts Health, Life, *Philip S. Chua* + + 20. Heart to Heart, Are We Getting Enough Sleep, *Philip S. Chua* + + 21. Heart to Heart, Obesity: A Killer, *Philip S. Chua* + + 22. Are we the disappearing breed of professionals in this country?, *Cesar D. Candari* + + 23. If You Dream It, Do It Retirement, *Cesar D. Candari* + + 24. Only In America, Human Interest Story, *Anonymous*

Writings 11 Book, August, 2011 + +

1. SONA In English and Filipino, *Pres. Benigno Aquino III (P-Noy)* + + 2. Telltale Signs: SONA and the Dogfight Over Spratlys, *Rodel Rodis* + + 3. Why China will not bring the Spratlys issue to the United Nations, *Ted Laguatan* + + 4. Random Thoughts, On Website Demise and On Disunity, *Tatay Jobo Elizes* + + 5. Can Local Private Sector Help Reverse Philippine's Migration Addiction?, *Jeremiah M. Opiniano* + + 6. What Fuels the Passion of Filipinos to Pursue Studies and Work in UK?, *Ofw Journalism Consortium* + + 7. Our Life in the Philippines, *Bob & Carol Hammerslag* + + 8. Reality Check: the Philippines – A Tropical Paradise for the Retiree?, *by Bob & Carol Hammerslag* + + 9. Filipinos Dominate Cruise Ships, *Roger P. Olivares* + + 10. Vargas: Hero, Villain, Tragic Figure?, *Roger P. Olivares* + + 11. Is it Hell to go Back Home?, *Roger P. Olivares* + + 12. The Filipino, now a commodity!, *Roger P. Olivares* + + 13. How US Can Create Jobs, *Rob Ceralvo* + + 14. Modus Operandi - Common Crimes (In Metro Manila, Philippines), *Anonymous* + + 15. Poem, Kabuhayang Bansa At Wika, *Irineo P. Goce (aka KaPule 2 and Leonidas Agbayani)* + + 16. Random Sayings & Advices, *Anonymous*

Writings 12 Book, 2012

1. Twenty Excuses Filipinos Use, *Orion Perez Dumdum* + + 2. One By One, The Petals Drop, *Julia C. Lagoc* + + 3. Religion & the Scientist, *Honorio M. Cruz, MD* + + 4. The Tales of the Aswang & Bangungot, *Honorio M. Cruz, MD* + + 5. Sex & Politics, *Honrio M. Cruz, MD* + + 6. Autopsy, *Ben Gonzales, MD* + + 7. Geekmocracy, *Mar-Vic Cagurangan* + + 8. Flights: Voice from the Future that Lives in the Past, *Mar-Vic Cagurangan* + + 9. Kaya Natin! Sanctuary, *Marisa Lerias* + + 10. The Days of Courage, *Gerry Partido* + + 11. Earth Day and the Tragedy of a Famous River, *Cesar D. Candari, MD, FCAP Emeritus* + + 12. Few Filipino-American Nonprofits Getting Political, *Erwin De Leon* + + 13. Filipino-American Political Invisibility And Community Organizations, *Erwin De Leon* I+ + 14. I'm 32 and I am still a Virgin, *Jovelyn Bayubay Revilla* + + 15. Hiding Ill-Gotten Wealth, *Jobo Elizes*

Solo Authored Books: + + +

Book A, **Turning Points - Empty Dreams**, *Job Elizes Sr,1968,Reissue 2009, 6x9,* + +
BookA2, **Turning Points - Empty Dreams**, *Job Elizes Sr, 1968,Reissue 2012, 5x8,* + +
Book B, **Be Considerate - Behaviour Issues**, *Tatay Jobo Elizes (Jr), 2009* + + +
Book C, **Piglets Unlimited - Wealth Untapped**, *Tatay Jobo Elizes, 2009* + + +
Book D, **Out of the Misty Sea We Must**, *Cesar Lumba, 2010* + + +
Book E, **Fulfilled** - *Gonzales Reynaldo, Editor, 2010* + + +

Dook F - **Reflections** - *Bert Guiang, 2010* + + +
Book G, **Writings 7 - My Vintage Pics**, *Tatay Jobo Elizes, 2010* + + +
Book H, **May Bagwis Ang Pag-ibig**, *Percival C. Cruz* + + +
Book I, **Letters To Matrimony**, *Irineo Perez Coce, Ka Pule2, 2011* + + +
Book J, **Songs I Wish You Knew**, *Soledad R. Juan, 2011* + + +

Book K, **Make My Day,** *Larry Henares Jr., 1993, Re-issue 2011* + + +
Book L, **Our Guerrero Family,** *Tatay Jobo Elizes, 2010* + + +
Book M, **Handy Jokes,** *Tatay J. Elizes, 2011* +
Book N, **FaveArt 1,** *Tatay Jobo Elizes, 2011* + +
Book O, **Beyond idle thoughts**, *MLMunoz, Sept,2011* + + +

Book P, **Cracks In The Armor**, *Mariano Ngan, Oct 2011* + + +
Book Q, **FaveArt 2**, *Tatay Jobo Elizes, 2011* + +
Book R, **Balitang Kutsero,** *Perry Diaz, Jan 2012* + + +
Book S, **FaveArt3,** *Tatay Jobo, 2011* + + +
Book T, **FaveArt4** *,2012, Tatay Jobo* + + +

Book U, **Stack Family Journals**, *Phil & Fe Stack, 2012* + + +
Book V, **Emily, An Adoption Journey**, *Romerl Elizes, 2012* + + +
Book W, **Hermes Alegre Art Gallery**, *TJ & Hermes, 2012* + + +
Book X, **Masaya Din, Malungkot Din,** *Jovelyn Bayubay Revilla, 2012* + + +
Book Y, **Tiis, Sipag At Tiyaga,** *Raquel Delfin Padilla, 2012* + + +

Book Z, **Until I Meet You,** *Jhackie Eslit Bayobay, 2012* + + +
Book AA, **Buhay At Pag-ibig**, *Argel Lucero Tamayo, 2012* + + +
Book AB, **Hail to the Second Best,** *Dr. Philip Stack, 2012* + + +
Book AC, **Life Bus,** *Mommy Joyce Pineda-Faulmino, 2012* + + +
Book AD, **My Candid Musings,** *Monette Dioquino Calugay, 2012* + + +

Book AE, **Tickets to Life,** *Maria Lourdes Jesalva, 2012* + + +
Book AF, **The Dove Files**, *Mike Portes, 2012* + +
Book AG, **Nursing Vignettes**, *Jocelyn Cerrudo Sese, 2012* + + +
Book AH, **Poor Ba Us,** *R.A. Gubalane, 2012* + +
Book AI, **Summer Idyll,** *Avelina Gil, 2012* + +

Book AJ, **Legacy (Pamana),** *Rachel Astrero, 2012* + + +

Please buy online at www.amazon.com *or* www.createspace.com *or give as gift in hard copy or kindle edition. All authors and titles are easy to search, trace or find online. Thanks. Self--Publisher Tatay Jobo Elizes (pic below)*

Philippine Scenic Places

Rizal Park, Manila, Phl

Old Govt Bldg, Now National Museum, Manila, Phl

Famous Bohol Chockolate Hills

Tourist House Boat, Somewhere, Phl

Famous Hundred Islands in Pangasinan Shores

Snorkeling in clear water, Somewhere, Phl

Mt. Banahaw, Quezon Province, Phl